MICHAEL PATERSON & LIZ CRUMLISH

Group Supervision

Notes for Beginners

The Institute of
Pastoral Supervision
& Reflective Practice

First published by IPSRP 2022

First edition

ISBN: 9798360035534

This book was professionally typeset on Reedsy.
Find out more at reedsy.com

Groups do not happen.
They are created and nurtured.
So too with books.
They don't happen.
They emerge out of story-shaped communities.

This book is dedicated to
the families who stand behind us,
the groups who stand beside us
and the world of practice
which stands before us.

Group supervision comes down to Plumbing, Poetry and Policing

Gaie Houston

Step by step the longest march
can be won, can be won.
Many stones can form an arch,
singly none, singly none.
And by union what we will
may be accomplished still.
Drops of water turn a mill,
singly none, singly none.

Pete Seeger

Contents

Foreword

If ever there was a time when we needed tools for harnessing our combined wisdom, it is now. Recent global catastrophes have stopped us in our tracks and brought to our collective awareness the stark reality that we live in a time of exponential change. We have spent the past number of years living in survival mode yearning for a return to 'normal' or at best a 'new normal'. Yet there is no new normal. No new paradigm to replace the old. Our environment is changing faster than we can adapt. Every species before us, that has lived in such a time, has gone extinct, or it has undergone a radical transformation. However, for the first time in the evolutionary process we are a species who can make the conscious choice, extinction or transformation.

This at a time when increasing numbers of us are on the move, fleeing persecution or poverty, simply seeking a fair share of our earth's resources. This is a time of existential crisis in which fear fuels the building of walls, the strengthening of borders, the search for security in fundamental certainties and the false safety of closed communities.

In the midst of this chaos no one community, profession or nation has all that we need to avert extinction. Having said that, together we can forge an alternative path. In their book Liz and Michael offer a not insubstantial contribution to this collective search. With a captivating title they set a rich context for: learning across professions through *group supervision*; with the attitude of openness to the emerging future *for beginners*; at the service of our shared future in *fostering the common good.*

We are all beginners on this adventure on which the emerging alternative to extinction is characterised by co-creation, maximum participation and imaginative transformation. These three capacities are amply manifest in the collaborative process that Michael and Liz set out on for this book, with colleagues from many contexts. They invite us now to join with them on the on-going journey as we make this book a living document guiding our reflexive conversations.

Personally, the experience of reading this book drew me into the potential of enhanced learning through vulnerability, routinely keeping it simple and allowing first names to make it an intimate journey. Surfing along between poetry, practice and theory brought to life the potential that is unleashed when choosing the reflexive turn is enhanced by a communal reflexive conversation.

Bringing the creativity, energy and imagination that we associate with Liz and Michael, both in their practice of facilitating learning and their previous written collaborations, makes it more likely that group reflexive conversations could be chosen as the best option for learning and insight and not simply to save time or money.

In the hands of Michael and Liz, 'supervision' becomes a word that is used to describe the intensely rich capacity when a group of human beings get together to make meaning. They address not only a gap in the literature but do so at a crucial moment given the contemporary struggles of the people of our time.

Thank you both!

Dr Bobby Moore

Author: *Reflexive Supervision: A workbook for learning within and across professions* (2017).

Preface

Supervision is all about conversations. Some of those conversations are external and interpersonal, others internal and undisclosed.

In writing this book we have held in mind those currently enrolled on the Institute's *Diploma in Group Supervision.* Seeing their faces around the training room, the dining table and the campfire leads us to write conversationally, addressing them directly and informally as our peers.

Because we want this book to be conversational we have intentionally abandoned third person academic writing to directly address you, dear reader. We have also accorded authors the dignity of their full names rather than their surnames alone. Since supervision is fundamentally about hospitality, according people their own names matters. Some of those cited are personal friends, others are friends by adoption and others wise guides who have taught and formed us. A profound bow to each and every one of them.

Our hope is that this book offers an introductory guide to group supervisors in training and a resource to dip into for those already working with groups. As such it sits alongside *Between a Rock and a Hard Place* (2020) which expounded our soul, role and context framework and *Pastoral Supervision: Creativity in Action* (2021) in which we offer a range of creative modalities.

In the interests of transparency, Michael is responsible for the text of the book and Liz for the poems and creative reflections.

The notes which follow are conversation starters. Please be in touch if you would like to pick up the conversation in a consultation, supervision group, workshop or training opportunity either in-person or online: training@ip-srp.org.uk

Acknowledgement

Without the friendship and continuous support of Bobby Moore this book would never have seen the light of day. Thanks too to our IPSRP colleagues Bob Whorton, Geoff Broughton, Ian Taylor, Lynnette Harborne, Markus Lange, Tony Nolan and to Bec Loundar of Alphacrucis University College for hearing us into speech and for critical friendship and ongoing reflexive conversations.

Especial thanks to Michael Carroll, Anna Chesner, Ger Holton, Ewan Kelly, Jane Leach, Bernd Leygraf, Teresa Robs, Wendy Robinson, Jessica Rose and Lia Zografou who taught us never to settle for anything less than transformative supervision.

A huge thank you to our students who tested this material as it was being written: Fiona, Ian, Jane B , Jane D, Janet, Lorraine and Paul.

To those who read, commented and made improving suggestions on various iterations of this book - Ed Vaughan, Geoff Broughton, Jane Bingham, Jo Sullivan, Kate Beer - and to Jessica Rose who typically went above and beyond in her detailed feedback, a very sincere thank you .

Thanks too to Linda and Lindsay whose island hospitality made the completion of this book possible.

And to Mario, Idris and Zara: no words can express our appreciation for consistently believing in us, feeding and watering us and forgiving our regular absences while writing.

Introduction

Supervision is a highly contested word with multiple and conflicting meanings.

Part One: Introducing Supervision argues that to be truly *super* and *visionary*, supervision engages Soul, Role and Context in dialogue. Distinctions are offered between supervision and other caring interventions. Cross-Professional supervision is introduced as a discipline in which the expertise of the supervisor is found not in holding pedigree status within a given discipline but rather in having the skills to facilitate reflexive conversations across disciplines. If you are new to supervision we recommend starting here.

Traditionally, training in Group Supervision begins by focusing on issues of group management and group dynamics i.e. on what distinguishes *group* supervision from *individual* supervision. *Part Two: Theory with a Light Touch* turns starting from otherness on its head: it locates group supervision within the 'story-shaped communities' and families which have formed us. An approach to supervision which begins in autobiography and in our families of origin is expounded. Those who are familiar with supervision and group dynamics might like to begin by reading this part of the book.

Part Three offers clarifications about a range of issues: Who comes to group supervision? What do they do when they get there? How many should be in the group? How long should sessions last? The benefits and challenges of group supervision are outlined, the role of the group supervisor explored and the particularities of team, organizational and peer supervision are discussed. Those who carry responsibility for rolling out supervision within organizations might like to begin in Part Three.

In *Part Four: Soulful Supervision* a series of short reflections are offered which underscore the values-based ethos and spirituality of supervision characterised by attention to resonance over relevance, reciprocity over dominance and mutuality over power games. This short section may appeal to experienced supervisors who wish to reconnect with the soul and spirit of supervision.

Part Five: Getting underway walks beginning supervisors through the journey with a new group of supervisees. Full of practical suggestions, it takes readers from ways of advertising group supervision, through a taster session to endings with groups. Suggestions are offered for contracting, exploring boundaries, structuring the group time and managing when stuck. Group dynamics are explored in four ways: dynamics arising from the supervisor's conduct; dynamics arising from the organizational context; dynamics arising between group members and dynamics arising out of the material that is brought to supervision. This part of the book offers material to drop into as needs and issues arise in practice.

Relentless Self-Care for supervisors forms the heart of *Part Six – Supporting yourself for the Task.* This section highlights the importance of attending to oneself before supervision sessions, during sessions and after sessions. Note taking, non-defensive hospitality and supervision on supervision are also explored in this final part of the book. These final notes will be of interest to those who know the truth of the adage: 'If you truly care about the state of the world, then take time to replenish your spirit. Self-care is not selfish. You cannot serve from an empty vessel.'

Vulnerable Exchange

Both step onto the dance floor
their smiles betraying nothing
of the turbulence that lies beneath
They connect,
sizing each other up:
Will I be held without being contained?
Will I be led without being corralled?
Will our steps be together
be they quick step or waltz?
Should we falter, is there space to manoeuvre
to regroup, reframe
and pick up from where we left off?
Will the boundaries provide safety
while allowing improvisation within?
These questions are not diminished
as they tentatively engage
following a rhythm
that they discover together
making sense of the steps
as the dance blossoms into life.
The questions are embraced
carried forward
as they commit to trust
and see where their stepping out together leads.

I

Part One Introducing Supervision

Note 1 Supervision in a Nutshell

In supervision, 'I' sees with compassion what 'Me' does in practice.
Sheila Ryan[1]

Supervision is a highly contested word. Some love it, some loathe it. From the Latin *super* (above) and *videre* (to see), it suggests a view from above; a panoramic view; or amplified vision.[2] Sadly the bad press it often receives stems from experiences that are neither super nor visionary. Supervision describes the dynamic process between three nouns, three verbs and three time zones.

> Soul, Role, Context
> + Connect, Reflect, Respond
> + Past, Present, Future
> = Supervision

Soul, Role, Context

The nouns of supervision are Soul, Role and Context.

- *Soul* refers to the practitioner's motivation or inner drive: the *why* which underpins their work.
- *Role* refers to the actual post (paid or voluntary) they hold.
- *Context* refers to the everyday realities, people and dynamics practitioners encounter in the work place.

Supervision is the intentional and ongoing facilitated conversation between all three. If the conversation is limited to soul then we are in the realms of spiritual accompaniment or careers guidance. If the conversation is limited to role then we are in the realms of line management or mentoring. And if the conversation is limited to context then we are in the realms of systemic analysis or executive coaching. Bringing all three nouns together, supervision asks: How is your soul finding expression in your role within your given context? In my experience job satisfaction is directly related to supervisees ability to find sufficient harmony between soul, role and context and burnout begins when the needs of one or more of the three are left unmet.[3]

Connect, Reflect, Respond

The verbs of supervision are connect, reflect and respond.

- At root supervision is relational and not a 'do it yourself' activity. It *connects* supervisees outwards (with the supervisor and other supervisees) and inwards (with their Soul and motivational 'why).
- It favours *reflecting* over reporting. Reporting is transactional. It transfers information from one party (the supervisee) to another (the supervisor). Reflection on the other hand, presses the pause button and engages curiosity in the search for meaning.
- What is found through reflection determines the r*esponse* that can be enacted, lived out, taken forward by supervisees after sessions.

Past, Present, Future

Supervision provides an opportunity to reflect in three different time zones.

- Reflecting on the *past* in the present for the sake of the future fosters *hindsight.*[4]
- Reflecting in the *present* for the sake of deeper meaning fosters *insight.*
- Reflecting on the *future* for the sake of informed action fosters *foresight.*

Supervision moves freely between these different time zones according to the needs of supervisees and their intentions. 'I did X at work and wonder if I missed something' leads supervision to focus on the past. 'There's something stirring right now as I talk about Y' invites supervision to focus in on the present. 'Next time Z comes round I want to respond differently' directs the supervisory gaze towards the future.

Keeping it simple

Being clear what group members can and cannot expect is a requirement of ethical practice. It also saves groups from bumps and potholes in the road. Connect, Reflect, Respond are the key words in advertising a supervision group.

Soul, Role, Context

Our wholeness is manifest in Trinity
The energy of our soul
Embraced within our role
Given freedom in our context
Each diminished
unless all can be allowed full expression
One might prop up another for a season
lending energy to sustain
Such is reality
But beauty consists in all three
Soul, role and context
being freed to realise
their full potential
creating balance and harmony
in life and work together.

Note 2 Supervising Across the Professions

'Even with the increase of supervision literature, supervision training and practice still appears to be largely bound to the counselling or psychotherapy orientation of the supervisor. Closed systems are being challenged in several ways .. each with their own sectarian (tribal) beliefs and assumptions.'

Brigid Proctor [1]

Supervision has traditionally been both tribal and hierarchical. Tribal in that, despite growing trends to draw on more than one theoretical framework or modality, most supervisors practice within a closed loop system i.e. counsellors supervise counsellors, teachers supervise teachers and pastors supervise pastors. Belonging to a 'tribe' secures supervisors' place and identity within their respective professions but, as we know from life more generally, maturity arises when we break out of our own echo chambers and engage in conversations with those from other tribes. Supervisors who are secure in their identities find this adventure enriching. Less secure supervisors find it threatening not least because working between tribes and across professional disciplines topples hierarchical structures and threatens their place in the pecking order.

Until very recently, supervision has been dominated by top down models which envisage a senior and usually more experienced practitioner meeting with a junior less experienced practitioner for the purposes of quality assurance, ethical compliance and professional development. Bernard and

Goodyear sum up that well-worn understanding of group supervision as follows:

> 'Group Supervision is the regular meeting of a group of supervisees to monitor the quality of their work, and to further their understanding of themselves as clinicians, of the clients with whom they work, and of service delivery in general. These supervisees are aided in achieving these goals by their supervisor(s) and by their feedback from and interactions with each other.'[2]

Within that uni-professional approach to group supervision, the expertise of the supervisor is grounded in inhabiting the same professional discipline as their supervisees. . In contrast, cross-professional supervision locates the supervisor's expertise not in the professional discipline from which supervisees come (nursing, social work etc.) but in knowing how to hold, manage and facilitate space for reflexive conversations in which two fields of expertise meet: the practice-based expertise of the supervisee and the facilitating expertise of the supervisor. In the non-sectarian world of cross-professional supervision, a pharmacist can therefore supervise a youth worker; a care assistant a police officer; a social worker a faith leader: not in the technical aspects of those professional disciplines but in hosting reflexive conversations which connect soul with role and context.

In arguing for a move away from working in our own professional silos to working cross-professionally I acknowledge the pioneering work of Michael Carroll, Ger Holton and Bobby Moore. Michael Carroll's work led him from counselling to coaching and to write extensively on supervision from a phenomenological perspective.[3] Ger Holton has pioneered Cross-Professional Supervision as a discipline in her own right and founded the Supervisors Association of Ireland on those terms.[4] Bobby Moore's *Reflexive Supervision: A workbook for learning within and across professions* (2017) is the singular most refreshing volume on supervision to have been published in the last decade. I owe a personal debt to each of them for challenging the therapeutic paradigm of supervisory models which have for too long been uncritically applied to other disciplines without first checking their underlying assumptions: assumptions about what it means to be human, what makes for human well-being, the place and value of human interaction etc.. Different disciplines have different values. In business the job needs to get done, in spiritual direction the relationship with God is paramount and in personal therapy the inner journey takes priority. Working cross-professionally can release supervisors from disappearing down the various uni-professional rabbit holes which lead 'I know what you mean because I have been there' kinds of thinking. Freed from self-validating echo chambers there is less occasion for dispensing advice, providing solutions or inadvertently shaming supervisees for their lack of knowledge or poor performance. This book unashamedly promotes cross-professional supervision as the norm in group supervision and offers enough theory and practical suggestions to allow a supervisor from any discipline to supervise a group composed of people from a variety of professional fields.

Keeping it simple

Uni-professional supervisors need to understand what supervisees are talking about to be of use to them. In contrast, cross-professional supervisors need to know how to foster reflection, harness the group's energy and support supervisees of any discipline to access their own wisdom. The locus of expertise for uni-professional supervisors lies in being familiar with the work being presented. The locus of expertise for the cross-professional supervisor lies in facilitating reflexive conversation.

Cross-Professional Supervision

I do not need to understand
For you are the expert in your context
And you do not need to explain
the things you already know well.
Exchanging information
does not deepen reflection.

Rather -
It is the careful Co-creation
of an hospitable space
that allows souls to meet
paving the way
for mutual learning.
And when you share
the core of who you are in your work
then we can begin together
to unravel the elements that collide
the light and the dark
the joy and the sorrow
the hope and the fear
finding touching points
out of which insight
for movement and growth
might be realised.

Note 3 When is Supervision not Supervision

'What you see and hear depends a good deal on where you are standing; it also depends on what sort of person you are.'
C.S Lewis [1]

Supervision is not the only show in town nor is it always the most appropriate response to a person's needs since the issues brought to supervision could well be taken to other helping spaces each of which would hear what is said through their own distinctive filters. An example.

> *'I know it is spring and the flowers are beginning to emerge after the winter. I know the days are growing longer. But ever since my mother died, I find this time of the year very difficult.' (Pat, Nurse in Age Care)*

Taken to counselling, the *Counsellor* hears those two sentences through an intrapersonal filter and might therefore inquire: 'Tell me about your relationship with your mother'; 'Are you in a similar or different place of difficulty than at this time last year?'; 'Is there anything holding you back to the past or preventing you living in the present?' Counselling invites a deep dive into the inner world of the bereaved person.

Taken to spiritual direction, the *Spiritual Director* hears those sentences through a spiritual filter and might therefore inquire: 'Where does this leave you with God?'; 'How does your spiritual practice relate to what you are living through just now?'; 'Is there anything in your wisdom tradition that you could call on to get through?' Spiritual direction invites the bereaved person to critically engage with whatever it is that sustains them or fails to sustain them from the inside.

Taken to line management, the *Line Manager* hears those sentences through a work lens. No matter how caring the line manager may be, the bottom line is that the job of nursing needs to be done and if Pat cannot do it then someone will have to. The line manager may therefore inquire: 'Are you being supported (or can we find some support for you) at this difficult time?;' 'Do you feel able to stay at work at the moment or do you need to take time off?'; 'Are there any adjustments we can make to ensure that the job gets done?'

The question 'where does that leave the supervisor?' leads us to the heart of what is distinctive about supervision in that

> Supervision supports the wellbeing of the worker and the wellbeing of those with whom they work.

Thus a supervisor may ask Pat 'How are your difficulties impacting on your work?' or 'How is what you are experiencing just now affecting your ability to care for your patients?' If the supervisor focused solely on Pat's well-being, then she would be adopting the role of a friend or carer whereas, if the supervisor pays attention to Pat's well-being *and* the well-being of those in Pat's care then the conversation may be termed supervisory. The attention paid to the absent other, the person(s) in the practitioner's care, is a key feature of supervision. For nurses, the absent other is likely to be their patients; for teachers, their students; for youth workers, their young people.[2] Put simply, the people outside the supervision room - the people to whom care is offered - need to be given due attention by the supervisor by asking how supervisee's difficulties may be impacting on them. Returning to the example above, Pat's difficulties following the death of her mother certainly need to be taken seriously. But so too do the needs of those in

Pat's care. Supervision attends to personal and professional circumstances without under or overvaluing either.

Supervision is a work-based conversation. Work forms the basis of the conversation and gives it its focus but there are other forms of work-based conversation which should not be confused with supervision.

When is Supervision not Supervision?

- When groups meet primarily for training or to initiate people into a profession. This is the realm of coaching or mentoring or professional development.
- When the therapeutic need of participants is given greater attention than reflection on practice. This is the realm of group therapy or critical incident debriefing.
- When participants meet primarily for operational planning. Although an element of reflective practice may be included in such gatherings, unless such reflection arises out of the actual practice of the participants rather than from the managerial or strategic needs of their leaders, operational planning cannot truly be deemed supervision.
- When the purpose of meeting together is primarily to share information and bring workers up to date. If information needs to be shared and/or discussed that should happen in team updates and not in supervision.
- When it exists primarily for networking purposes and for getting to know who and what is out there. Supervision deals with specific issues as they arise in supervisee's practice. It does not trade in seminar topics, themes or topics for general discussion.
- When it exists primarily to manage poor performance, incompetence or dysfunctional individuals or teams.

Keeping it simple

Supervision facilitates work-based conversations which take the well-being of workers and those in their care seriously. Supervision cares for the supervisees in the room as much as for those outside of the room with whom they work. Being clear about the character of the group meeting allows those present to participate appropriately. Don't mix everything to do with groups into supervision.

On the carpet

The relief
when we realise
that there is a space
where it all matters
where we no longer have to edit out
parts of who we are
to prove our competence
or demonstrate our resilience
where we can own our doubts
and confess our fears
where we can celebrate fulfilment
and acknowledge longing
The carpet of supervision
has space for us to lay out our stories
and discover in the warp and weft
the colour and the vibrancy
the worn and the tired
and the wings that have carried us
on journeys near and far
Those wings that are simply resting after flight
and those that have been trodden on once too often
and now lie discarded and broken
There is space for all of it

And opportunity for us to sift,
regarding each piece carefully
Choosing what still belongs
in the next chapter of our story
and what we will bravely leave behind
moving on with a lightness
borne out of the task
of pausing to reflect.

II

Part Two Theory worn lightly

Note 4 Supervision Begins in Community

'Our lives are formed in story-shaped communities'
Stanley Hauerwas[1]

Notwithstanding Gaie Houston's *Red Book of Groups* (1993) and Brigid Proctor's *Group Supervision: A Guide to Creative Practice* (2008), writing on group supervision, is typically relegated to a chapter or two in larger volumes whose primary focus is on individual supervision.[2] Within those stand-alone chapters, what tends to be offered are adaptations of individual supervision to which is added material on group management and group dynamics. Almost invariably such books enumerate the economic and multi-perspectival benefits of group supervision. While not wishing to denigrate those publications or deny such claims, this book arises from a very different place and makes a simple plea: Let's tell a better story about group supervision. Let's tell a story that starts not in arguments based in economy (more people supervised in less time) or in multiplicity of insights (more participants results in a wider range of perspectives): rather let's tell a story about group supervision that finds its roots in the joys and hopes, the stresses and strains, the glories and challenges of life in community. Let's tell a story that roots group supervision in the incontrovertible truths that

> We were born in community. We live our lives in community. We die in community.

And let's tell a story that is honest enough to admit that life in community - whether at local level (with neighbours), at professional level (with colleagues), or at political level (the life of a nation) – is hard work and requires continuous renegotiation.

If the global Coronavirus pandemic taught us anything, it was surely this: that our lives are inextricably linked and that we impact and are impacted by one another. Why else did we observe lockdown? Why else did we wear masks? Why else did we develop vaccines if not for the truth that our lives are woven together and that our behaviours and values, our freedoms and responsibilities impact on each other.

Community life in the pandemic was marked by three phases. At the beginning, we were all in it together. We adjusted and adapted, complied and obeyed to get through as best we could. Here, in the UK, we stood at our front doors Thursday by Thursday clapping for our front line workers. We shopped for each other, looked out for each other and felt connected to each other. The changes we experienced interpersonally were reflected in the world of industry as car manufacturers switched to making ventilators, fashion designers knocked out PPE[3] and restaurateurs fed those on the breadline. Brought to our collective knees, we discovered that community does in fact exist, that there really is a thing called 'society'[4] and that despite our best efforts to live privatized lives, even in suburbia and dormitory towns, no man or woman is an island.

> We are each other's wind resistance and we will not make it on our own[5]

In phase two of the pandemic, we witnessed the breakdown of community spirit. Being 'in it together' gave way to the blame game. Covid-19 was the Chinese disease. It was a western conspiracy. Rising death tolls were the government's fault. Face masks were in short supply. Vaccines took too long to roll out. Fingers wagged, tempers flared, keyboard warriors typed furiously. Among those who dreamt that the virus might wake us up to who and how we are together, hopes were dashed. Community transitioned from being the place of healing to the place of wounding as self-interest displaced the common good and individuals' rights to party, or travel or gather in large groups sidelined the sense of being collectively responsible for each other's well-being.

Covid phase three was ushered in by governments who feared the public would revolt if they dared to introduce any further compliance measures. Infection rates continued to rise but the new message was 'every man, woman and child for themselves'. A.Y.O.R. living - life 'at your own risk' - became the new normal.

> It was the best of times, it was the worst of times.[6]

Responses to Covid-19 showed the human community at its very best and its very worst. Nevertheless, it would be naïve to canonize the behaviours of one sector of society and demonize the other since attitudes towards authority, rules and rule makers were already firmly set in the family – our primary community – long before the onset of Covid-19. Rules set by those who clearly loved us and had our best interests at heart had most chance of being taken seriously. Conversely, rules set by those who were inconsistent in their care for us, who were psychologically or emotionally absent were more likely to be distrusted and flouted. Those who grew up in ambivalent environments, quickly learned that survival entailed finely balancing sufficient compliance to remain 'under the radar' with just enough self-determination to stay out of harm's way.

> Underneath the behaviour is a feeling. Under the feeling is a need.
> Beyond the need is a longing to belong, to feel safe and to be seen.[7]

As we grow up and leave home, we spend our lives in 'repeating cycles of belonging and unbelonging'[8] of trying to fit in and of fearing being swallowed up; of hoping groups will be safe enough to be part of and fearing they will tear us apart. We join and leave nurseries, schools, friendship circles, relationships, jobs, clubs and societies. And when we find belonging challenging, we may avoid it altogether by becoming leaders of groups to which we never really belong.

Over the years I have worked with several supervisees who are leaders of groups they would never join. I think of pastors who lead churches they would not be seen dead in; social workers who lead teams they would want no part in and therapists who are utterly disparaging of the parent organizations which employ them. Leading as a way of avoiding belonging is one way of reducing the risk of being excluded. So too is leading to ensure that everyone loves you, appreciates you, thanks you and validates you. Neither are healthy. Neither are free. Neither are hospitable. Neither will make for a satisfactory supervisory experience.

Life in community is complex. Interacting with groups is complex. When everyone pulls together the sense of achievement is immense and 'restores faith in humanity'. Think of how people pull together around a common cause whether that be humanitarian aid for Ukraine, care for those affected by flash floods and bush fires in Australia or sponsoring the local child who needs emergency medical care. Pulling together touches deep into the soul. For all the dynamics involved, for all the foibles of the various characters we have to contend with, there is something deeply restorative about supervision in a group of people who get us, have our back and want to see us flourish. Supervision begins in community. Supervision happens in community and supervision sends us back out to heal and mend the broken communities in which we serve.

Keeping it simple

Those who supervise groups owe it to those who join them to have thought about their relationships with groups. What impact might it have on the group you run if you think it is only a cheaper and time saving option? And what difference could it make if you were to hold out for group supervision as the norm because it helps us live better and more fully in community and in society?

Telling a better story

There will always be those who tell us No!
Who like to wrap things up in jargon and complexity
Who are defenders of the mystery
keeping the simplicity of truth veiled and out of sight
Treat them with the respect they deserve
But find another way in
Perhaps a more circuitous route
involving a journey that gathers companions along the way
whose lighter steps resound in harmony
clearing a path for those who come after
and whose commitment to inclusion
unravels the cords of exclusion
Find a way
To break down the resistance
To dismantle the prejudice
To recover the hospitality
that is invitational and spacious
rooting experience in practice
Find a way that, despite the complexity,
hosts a space that is focused on being in community
reflecting on the work in hand for communal good
and that carries the label
"You, all of you, are welcome here."

Note 5 Who you are is why you supervise

'We are always coming from our autobiography.
Our own autobiography plays out in our work,
the career choices we make, the models with which we resonate,
the people with whom we work.'
Keemar Keemar[1]

In Full Spectrum Supervision (2013) Edna Murdoch and Jackie Arnold make the provocative claim: 'Who you are is *how* you supervise'.[2] In that short sentence, the *who* and the *how* of supervision are wedded together. Their claim flies in the face of those who say:

> 'I supervise as I was trained. I did a course in counselling supervision, pastoral supervision, art-therapy supervision and that is how I supervise.'

To such supervisors, the link between identity and performance is irrelevant. They studied supervisory frameworks, learned how to structure sessions and acquired a toolkit of modalities with which to work. 'I supervise as I was taught' they reply, 'of course my personality and unique individuality come into the mix, but fundamentally I supervise as I was trained'.

My first training was in counselling supervision. Having logged 450 hours of therapeutic client work, I went on to train as a supervisor for counsellors.

Inskipp and Proctor's three legged stool,[3] Hawkins and Shohet's seven eyes[4] and Page and Wosket's Cyclical Model[5] provided the building blocks for my support of others. Invariably the format of supervision sessions was case presentation and review. Month by month, practitioners showed up, told me how many clients they had, focused in on the trickier aspects of their practice and gave an overview of the rest. True to my training, my locus of expertise in offering supervision was fundamentally rooted in my experience as a practicing counsellor. Belonging to the same professional discipline grounded me and legitimated my efforts as a supervisor.

A decade later my perspective had changed. Teased by Val Wosket's remark that the issues of more mature practitioners are fundamentally their own issues,[6] I came to realise that the locus of my expertise as a supervisor lay much more in who I was as a person, i.e. in my identity than in my credentials as an experienced counsellor. To paraphrase Edna Murdoch and Jackie Arnold, I came to realise that who I am is not only *how* I supervise but more fundamentally, *why* I supervise. Let me illustrate from personal experience.

> Who you are is *why* you supervise.

I was born in Belfast, a city torn down the middle by division. The place of my birth - the Falls Road – is synonymous with 'The Troubles'. My first name 'Michael' establishes my catholic credentials. My surname 'Paterson' aligns me with protestant émigrés who fled to Scotland in search of food and work. Growing up, I spent my early years in a military family constantly on the move across Europe adapting to new circumstances every eighteen months, utterly dependent on my father's latest posting. Within months of settling back in Scotland, I was abused by a friend of my family. In one afternoon my innocence abruptly ended and a twenty year silence and deep hiding began. Fast forward to my first meeting with a psychotherapist who made me welcome, listened as I broke my silence and then pronounced the deepest of all benedictions: 'I believe you'. In those three words, and in the depth of compassion from which they came, my healing began.

It comes as no surprise, looking back, that my professional life has been lived in the space between: working with individuals and organizations who are internally conflicted, eliciting the voices of those who struggle to be heard, challenging unaccountable abuses of power and relentlessly pushing back at what is offered as professional wisdom.

My life as a psychotherapist, priest and supervisor was shaped in a whole series of communities long before I ever heard of Jung, Kung or Carroll:[7] the torn community of Belfast which gave me a passion for reconciliation; the resilient community of the Armed Forces which taught me to adapt and live an agile life; the fractured community of family which taught me never to presume or abuse another person's trust; the unaccountable and boundary-challenged community of church. Since 'family is the deepest pattern-maker for the rest of our lives',[8] I, like so many others in the caring professions, needed supervision long before I knew the term.

For the past twenty five years supervision has been the constant in my professional life both as a supervisee and as a supervisor. Who I am has been forged in multiple story-shaped communities. In some I have thrived. In others I have withered. In both, supervision has provided a consistent and ongoing brave space for the tough work of telling and facing the truth of my practice as my soul has sought to find expression in its role in various contexts.

Murdoch and Jackie Arnold are right: 'who I am is *how* I supervise.' But that's only the beginning of a much deeper and unfolding story which leads me to claim: 'who I am is *why* I supervise.' My hope is that you too can say that of your own practice as, together, we relocate our supervisory authority, not in tools and techniques but in harvesting the grit and the grace in our autobiographies, coming out from behind our professional masks and making ourselves available for the transformative work to which we are called.

Keeping it simple

Knowing how histories have shaped our career choices and the voluntary work we do, can be both informative and insightful for supervisors and for supervisees. Supervisors who can look inwards and know what has shaped and formed them take up less room in the supervisory space. Supervisors who don't, risk using groups to meet unmet personal needs. Befriending your history will enable others to do likewise.

Weaving

Laying down the warp
Those foundational elements
that stand alone
pronouncing contradiction
complimenting
contrasting
unconnected
tethered
fragile
robust
deliberate
accidental
waiting for the weft
that draws together the loose ends
to fashion a new creation
unique
yet containing the echoes
of past, present and future
in a glorious weaving of wonder
a gathering up
that becomes
a token of transition
for onward travel
informing yet not dictating the future
into which we are invited to weave
new threads of insight every day.

Note 6 Family Echoes in Groups

Every group carries within it echoes of our families of origin.
Bert Hellinger[1]

Every group carries an echo of our family of origin and every group carries echoes of previous groups with which we have engaged. Some echoes are audible, many are not. Faced with new groups we may find ourselves oscillating between wanting to belong and fearing losing our individuality. We wonder whether we will find people like us or be pushed out to the edge because we are different.[2] Like sniffer dogs we are alert to the scent of power and wonder how it will play out. In some groups our arrival is almost imperceptible, in other groups a fanfare heralds our entrance.

Those of us who supervise who were formed, nurtured and given the wings to fly in our families of origin may approach groups without much thought. Our early family pattern may make trust our default setting, after all, what is there to fear when you expect to find your place and voice in a group? Of such John Whittington writes:

> *'You can quickly sense when you meet someone who has a clear and robust sense of belonging in their family of origin. You can feel they are grounded in themselves [they] embody a calm yet vital energy. They have plenty of resources that they can offer to others, but they know and respect the boundaries of those offers and are self-contained, resourced from within.'*[3]

Thankfully some such people find their ways into supervision but, truth be told, they are in the minority. In my experience, the majority of supervisors and supervisees, are works-in-progress, courageous folk who have had to overcome hurdles in their lives, hurdles which led them to seek help at some point in their lives and then, later, to train as practitioners for those helping professions.

> Every group simultaneously carries the twin possibilities of repair and repeat of our original family dynamic.

If every group carries echoes of our families of origin then every group simultaneously carries the twin possibilities of repairing and repeating our original family dynamics.

Those who are hoping for a reparative experience - the chance to repair earlier experiences - may approach groups gingerly and through tentative and incremental acts of trust, discover the grace of acceptance, of being allowed to be themselves and of tasting the joyous freedom that comes from belonging.

Those who approach groups expecting them to repeat old familiar patterns of exclusion and rejection, may struggle to find groups worthwhile and, fearing rejection, may either refuse to join a group or be deeply ambivalent in their participation and group interaction. The problem of course arises when neither belonging nor refusal to participate are optional. Whereas a person can choose whether or not to join the Parent Teacher Association or accept the invitation to serve on a charitable committee, when it comes to earning a living – or indeed to training as a supervisor - few have any choice over their colleagues, co-workers or peers. Those who have managed to cut through the binary patterns of repeat and repair will be able to approach such groups for what they are - groups in their own right with their own patterns of interaction rather than theatres in which old family (and previous group) dramas are incessantly replayed.

> If we do not transform our pain we will surely transmit it to those around us and risk carrying it from group to group.

In *Systemic Coaching & Constellations*, John Whittington identifies several ways in which material that has not been transformed or integrated from our early lives can become internalised and replayed over and over again in our working lives. What he says of coaches is equally applicable to supervisors.

> *'You were recruited by family members to help resolve their conflict. You became a peacemaker as a child or young adult. Perhaps you bring that familiar pattern into your work...*
>
> *You rejected the authority of one or both parents and that leaves you with a difficulty finding your own [authority] or allowing others to lead you.*
>
> *You tried to carry one parent's pain, depression or anxiety and this carrying stays with you as you go into the world of work and eventually, coaching.*
>
> *You hold a semi-conscious and private wish that you could have saved, rescued or healed someone (or everyone) in your family of origin. You become a coach and bring this yearning with you.*
>
> *Your parents recruited you to take care of them in some subtle or more explicit ways. In this way you learnt to be helpful from early on, but from a level in the system that was not yours.*
>
> *You didn't feel you received what you needed as a child, so you give and give in the unconscious hope of receiving what was not available...'*

The unresolved material we each carry from our childhood patterning is of deep significance since,

> 'we are drawn towards the comfort of familiar pain time and again, until we see the pattern underneath.'[4]

Knowing and being reconciled to their own family of origin stories enables supervisors to offer *other*-centred hospitality to group members and frees group participants from being unconsciously recruited to repeating or repairing deficits in the supervisor's early history. And when groups are allowed to be 'other' - rather than family echo chambers - then supervisors are freed from having to re-enact old behaviours. Thus supervisors who inherited life scripts about being put down in their families of origin become able to assume their appropriate size in groups without overplaying or underplaying their roles.

The consequences for practice are considerable since supervisors who are deeply familiar with their own stories and attend to their deficits in personal rather than professional spaces, have sufficient internal space to notice how group members take their place in groups: noticing those who effortlessly glide into the group environment and make it their own and those who loiter at the door or sit with their videos and microphones off online waiting to be invited in. So too, supervisors who know and have come to terms with their own early patterning have room to be simply curious (without making comparisons) about those who struggle to say hello and join groups and those who have difficulty saying goodbye and leaving.

Supervisors owe it to their supervisees to be actively working at becoming free, unhindered and unencumbered from patterns and scripts set in childhood, family life and previous groups. Becoming free enables supervisors to show up more fully, take up less space and facilitate deeper explorations. Whether they like it or not, supervisors model professional personas, attitudes and values. We owe it to those who want to get real with us to get real with ourselves. Let our work be characterised by repair more than repeat and when we get the balance wrong - as surely we will - let the repair cycle begin once again.

Keeping it simple

Every group carries echoes of our families of origin. Expecting the supervisory space to amplify some echoes and turn down the volume of others enables the group supervisor to stick to the task of facilitating reflection and not repairing the family tree. To do that supervisors need to be working to break their own binary cycles of repeat and repair.

Breaking out

Shall I be defined
by the cocoon in which I was formed
Destined to repeat a pattern
predictable and known
Or might I tentatively anticipate change
Finding wings that flex
and antennae that chart a way to be free
Is it worth risking the unknown
Or shall I stick with the tried and tested
that have sustained me so far
Grit and determination have helped me survive
Might courage and imagination be my companions
as I flirt with the vulnerability of being seen
in an unfamiliar space.
Perhaps it's time to lay down the old and familiar
to brave an encounter with uncharted potential
that hints at the possibility of growth
in the uncertainty that is the future.

Note 7 Integrated and Unresolved Family Echoes in Groups

'We are about as effective as stopping an emotion as we are at preventing a sneeze.'
Antonio Damasio[1]

'We are about as effective as stopping an emotion as we are at preventing a sneeze.' The same can be said about stopping echoes of families of origin reverberating around the supervisory space. We cannot stop them but we can learn to know which of them are old friends we can greet and let go of, and which are demons that are likely to jump up and bite us unless we face them head on.

In group supervision, what has not been owned may take ownership of the group and what has not been integrated may infect group interactions. Common symptoms of unresolved material arising from participants' families of origin are behaviours and interactions characterised by the verbs repeat, react, retaliate.

Unresolved family echoes

Repeat

Groups have a tendency to repeat old family patterns that participants – supervisors and supervisees alike – hope is done and dusted and consigned to the past. A personal example:

I joined a supervision group at a time of crisis personally and professionally. I arrived early, found the venue and then walked slowly around the block so as to arrive just on time. Within minutes of crossing the threshold I found myself drowning in a sea of twelve people all clamouring for the supervisor's attention. It was as if the room had the word 'repeat' in neon lights emblazoned on the walls. Familiar childhood feelings of being squeezed out, voiceless and rendered invisible returned unbidden. Unable to bear the pain of repeat I left the group at the interval never to return.

React

Groups in which participants react rather than reflect may struggle with the task of supervision.

One care agency in which I supervised turned reaction into an art form. No matter how much notice I gave about the date, time and place of supervision, no matter the lengths I went to ring fence the space, ensure shifts were covered, some urgent drama or pressing issue inevitably cropped up and sabotaged supervision from taking place. Given that organizations often mirror the lives of those for whom they exist, it was hardly surprising that the staff had got caught in the cycles of interruption and reactive response that characterised the lives of the children in their care.

Retaliate

Retaliate is a word likely to raise some eyebrows in a book about supervision. Surely supervisors and supervisees are sufficiently well-behaved to prevent retaliation happening in supervision? Yes and no. Among groups comprised of those who have willingly signed up for supervision, retaliation and its cousin, revenge are unlikely.[2] But among groups in which participation or, more precisely, attendance is compulsory, then a whole range of ugly dynamics arising from childhood may be displayed.

In one group of nurses I supervised, an otherwise compassionate and highly professional participant spent the whole session unwittingly persecuting her colleagues and baiting them to retaliate. I later learned that in her family, the only way to get noticed was to outdo violence with violence. Her tongue was her sharpest and most dangerous weapon.

Integrated family echoes

Just as disowned and homeless aspects of personal history may manifest in group interactions so too what has been integrated from supervisees' families of origin may be expressed in group behaviours and interactions characterised by the verbs repair, reflect, rehearse, revise.

Repair

When supervisors balance leadership and autonomy, early childhood patterns about how to be in groups may well be repaired without anyone realizing it. Even without knowing the details of group members lives, sensitive supervisors operate from the premise that it is their responsibility to give the group reasons to trust them rather than the group's responsibility to trust the supervisor. Paying careful attention to all present and not to the favoured or the notorious, sets the reparative process in motion. Supervisors who know that they cannot change the group's purpose from reflection-on-practice to family therapy, ensure that the group is neither idealized (this is the only place I can be myself) nor weaponized (if I can't be heard here there is nowhere left for me to go).

Reflect

In contrast to organizations which avoid reflecting by constantly reacting and responding to crisis after crisis, supervisors from families which regularly stopped to consider options, in which voices and viewpoints were elicited and competing needs attended to, will have learned the value of pausing between event and response. The reflective turn will have become instilled in such practitioners who will instinctively pause before responding. Reflection is the bread and butter of supervision. Myriad are the obstacles to pursuing it in group supervision.

Rehearse

Supervisees from families where play and imagination were encouraged may well find in group supervision an invaluable opportunity for rehearsal and experimentation. Sometimes rehearsal takes the form of trying out a different role or way of being. Someone caught, for example, in the dynamics of the drama triangle[3] might experiment with being caring without being a rescuer, or being assertive without being persecutory or appropriately vulnerable without playing the victim. Supervision groups which offer participants sufficient safety to widen their repertoire of default and uncritically adopted responses can be invaluable not only in helping practitioners with their immediate professional issues but in expanding their role repertoire and responses in life more generally.[4]

Re-vision

Supervision groups which bear the hallmark of re-vision are those in which participants do not have to explain themselves or spend precious time bringing others up to speed with what they themselves know and experience. Re-vision groups are those in which participants can drop into whatever aspect of soul, role and context is uppermost for them at any given time without feeling the need to take care of others' sensibilities, pet theories or hypotheses. One of the extraordinary graces of a group in which re-visioning is possible is that people find the wings to fly irrespective of what others in the group think. Such groups are freeing beyond measure and most likely to be populated by participants who have had to reinvent themselves in response to hard knocks in life.

Keeping it simple

Supervisors are not family therapists and even those who are should stick to hosting work-based reflexive conversations when supervising. Participants' pre-histories will be in the room for sure but that does not mean they have to become the focus of the session. Simple questions at the groups first meeting such as the following can elicit enough material to be getting on with: 'If this group behaved like your family what would happen?' 'If in the life of this group you were to adopt a different role than the one you played in your family what difference would that make to you being here?'

Unfiltered offering

What a difference it makes
when we can bring our whole selves
into conversation about our work.
Not just the parts we think are acceptable
Not just the bits we've managed to knock into shape
But an opportunity, in conversation
to reflect on the professional
and the unprofessional part of self
Releasing the emotions we keep carefully hidden
as we practice our craft
Like breathing out
after the photo has been taken
repairing, reflecting, rehearsing, revising
Supervision is a chance to be real
to step off the pristine path
and forage in the weeds
to catch a glimpse
of things forgotten
or hidden out of sight
hauling them back into the light
so that we might poke and prod
and welcome those parts of our selves
that speak of both growth and potential
of a work in progress.
Doing that work, in community
keeps us real
as we continue to give of ourselves
for the sake of the other.

Note 8 The Effective Group Supervisor

And the one throwing the lifebelt, even he needs help at times:
Stranded on the beach terrified of the waves.
Brian Patten[1]

When it comes to group supervision, especially in the early days, it is important to notice what gets triggered in the fledgling supervisor and in the newly established group. Marie-Louise Ögren writes:

> *On the part of the supervisees, a wish to be seen and confirmed sparks early emotional needs and can easily create a strong dependency or its opposite in the form of an active distance-taking stance as a shield against closeness and dependency.*[2]

Supervisors-in-training should also be aware of their corresponding needs to be confirmed not only by group members but also by their course tutors, their peers and their supervisors - needs that sometimes can contradict each other.

Becoming sufficiently self-aware that inner drivers can be revealed and personal needs met in personal rather than professional places is one of the hallmarks of effective supervision. As a young child, it is age appropriate to react instinctively to being told what to do. But if at forty, we are still acting out of our un-reflective childhood programming then we are in trouble. Supervisors who can provide age and stage appropriate modelling, who can embody role authority without being rule bound have an important role to play in supervisees' lives.

As we have seen, effective supervision has a strongly reparative dimension in which deficits can be met with compassion and *re*-sourcing needs can be addressed. In well run groups, supervisees who are uncritically compliant, who never question what is said by those in authority can learn to find their own voice and supervisory style. Likewise, those who are instinctively anarchic, who have no room for others' points of view can learn to suspend judgment and weigh up what is offered to them.

> Effective supervisors foster supervisees' autonomy. Ineffective supervisors replicate themselves.

Effective group supervision fosters the unique individuality of each practitioner and supports autonomous practice. It recognises the value that each party – supervisor and supervisee – brings to the encounter and in so doing is deeply respectful of the ways in which participants' personal histories are manifest and played out in the supervisory space. By contrast, ineffective supervision attempts to replicate the style, voice, thinking and modalities of the supervisor. Supervisors who see their role as dispensers of wisdom keep supervisees dependent and create relationships which are hierarchical.

> Supervision is rooted in autobiography, not in frameworks, tools and techniques.

If, as this book claims, group supervision is rooted not in frameworks, tools and techniques but in the messiness of life in community, then surely training to supervise groups requires more rigorous preparation than a day added on to a curriculum packed individual supervision course or a chapter in an otherwise comprehensive supervision text book.

Traditionally the starting place in the literature of group supervision is with group participants: hence the emphasis on group management and group dynamics. This book rewinds the clock and argues that if you want to go forward you have to first look backwards.[3]

That supervision begins in autobiography is foundational to the *better story* this book is advocating: the stories we supervisors have inherited about our beginnings; the stories we tell about our lives; and the continuously redacted stories we use to present ourselves to the world of work. Our stories may be deeply buried or worn on our sleeves. They may be consigned to silence or heralded from the rooftops.

> Our lives are lived in search of a narrator.

Either way, our lives are lived 'in search of a narrator'[4] and if we do not narrate our own lives, if we do not actively decide how the story goes, then we can be sure that the scripts that were drafted for us in childhood will effortlessly narrate our lives for us. Those of us who facilitate group supervision owe it to our supervisees to become active narrators of our own stories since knowing and owning our stories enables us to really show up for our supervisees and not use groups to meet our own needs. We do *not* have to be fully 'sorted' but we *do* need to be able to bring into 'compassionate conscious awareness'[5] those aspects of our past that are likely to impair the quality of hospitality and presence we offer others in supervision.

Extending compassion towards ourselves allows us to recognize that 'instead of trying to resist, deny or fight what we are carrying from the past' we can see our past 'as a doorway into another level of understanding and insight'.[6] In other words, the bruises and wounds we have acquired over the years, if actively addressed don't have to be obstacles to the work we do but may in fact turn out to be deepest resources we have for our work with others.

> Wounded healers can do immense good. Leaking wounders can do immense harm.

And if our wounds are out of awareness and we simply do not know we have them, then we can be sure that supervisees will bring them to our doors for our full undivided attention.

Keeping it simple

If supervision is all about fostering autonomy and practitioner identity then why worry about getting it right? Be authentic. Be resourced by your wounds - not dragged down by them. Whatever the scripts others have written for you, the way the plot unfolds from here on is in your hands. Model that for your supervisees and empowerment will follow.

Transformative

Transforming wisdom
Bringing the hidden into the light
Making the unseen visible
Ceaselessly revealing what is beautiful and true
Calling forth what is tentative to reveal conviction
Breathing power into vulnerability
releasing truth and goodness and insight
Gently unveiling hopes and longings
carefully protected from the harsh light of judgment
Encouraging dreams to emerge
and be entered into playfully
creatively nurtured and sustained
by wisdom that does not diminish but enhances all that is
Mobilising tiny steps of possibility
into leaps of adventure
fuelled by risk
made possible by reflecting
in a space characterised by
attentive accompaniment
and careful containment:
the space of transformative supervision.

Note 9 Stages of Group Life

'Supervision groups need often to be a good home for their members – not an ideal or idealized home but one where there can be comfort and honesty, some love and loyalty and the exchanging from time to time of home truths.'

Gaie Houston[1]

The life cycle of groups has been ably mapped by Bruce Tuckman et al.[2] The stages they outline of Forming, Storming, Norming, Performing and Mourning are descriptive rather than linear. Rare is the group which proceeds from forming to mourning without the turbulence of storming not simply at stage two but at any stage in its life together.

Tuckman (1965) Group Stages	*Schutz (1973) Developmental Needs*	*Bion (1961) Basic Assumptions*
Forming	Inclusion/Exclusion	Dependency
Storming	Assertion/Authority	Flight/Flight
Norming	Affection	Pairing
Performing	Achievement	Work Group
Mourning	Closing	

Peter Hawkins and Aisling McMahon (2020) link Bruce Tuckman's stages of group life to William Schutz's categorization of developmental needs[3] and Wilfrid Bion's group assumptions[4] as outlined in Table 1.

Hatches

Hatches asks about the origins, birth or genesis of a group.

- What is the group's birthing story?
- Who were the parents?
- Was the birth of the group planned or unexpected?
- Who carried the group in its infancy?
- Who laboured for it?
- Who brought it to birth?
- How does the group's birth story or genesis get played out in the group's internal dynamic?

Matches

Remembering Wilfrid Bion's insight that on entering a new group, participants will often seek out someone like them

- What are the pairings or twinnings in the group?
- Who are your next of kin in the group?
- Who are your distant cousins?
- Who in the group is not a bit like you?
- Which group members form the working group and which constitute the basic assumption group? (Bion)[5]
- Who are the singletons or the overly needy who want to be everyone's friend?
- And what effect do the matches and (failed matches) have on the life of the group?

Scratches

Life in community inevitably has its ups and downs but how those are handled reveals a lot about the ethos, values and behaviours of groups. Reflecting at the review point of a group, perhaps after four or five sessions, participants could be invited to ask:

- Who are the groups guardians, parents or responsible adults?
- What dynamic do they bring to the group?
- When things go wrong who does the soothing?
- Who protects the group and keeps it from harm?
- Who takes it on themselves to feed and nurture the group?
- Who are the habitual takers and who are the habitual givers?
- Who lies awake at night worrying about the group?
- Who carries the group conscience?

Dispatches

Endings are revealed in plain sight in every group session in which hints are given about final endings. I would encourage beginning supervisors to consider endings long before a group member leaves or the group itself completes its work together. The following questions may reveal a lot about what is happening in group life:

- What dynamic does absence play in absorbing the group's attention?
- Who struggles to say hello and who struggles to say goodbye in this group?
- Whose sense of rejection is triggered when group members don't show up or are late or absent themselves early?
- Whose attendance is irregular?
- Whose presence feels like absence?
- Who threatens the group by talk of leaving?
- In what ways does the group dispatch, dismiss, or ostracize the supervisor?
- How does the group manage planned and unplanned exits?
- How does the group in effect dispatch those who won't play ball?
- How does the group face up to or deny its own ending?

If the roots of group supervision lie in the story-shaped communities of all who participate, then it is also true that the group itself will be a multi-storied community. Knowing and naming that story invites collaborative and co-creative story lines for how the group chooses to be. Beginning supervisors need to beware of getting so caught up in the stories that group members bring to the session that they miss the story that the group is telling about itself.

Keeping it simple

Every group has a story but don't mistake a story for a predetermined programme. Healthy groups write their own creative stories. Healthy supervisors become part of the plot. Unhealthy groups look for ready-made templates. Unhealthy supervisors put ticks in spreadsheets.

Hatches, matches, scratches, dispatches

None of us arrives in group space
as pristine blank canvases
We all carry with us experiences that have helped us grow
alongside encounters that make us wary
As we pour these into what we create together
we begin to fuse together light and dark
and a multi hued palette emerges.
Sometimes the colours blend
At other times they clash.
It takes patience
and courage
hard work
and determination
to find a way of working together
that has space to acknowledge darkness
without extinguishing the light
and to embark on a shared endeavour
of contributing to a new collaborative work.

Note 10 Difference and Diversity in Groups

'Supervision is a container for creativity and chaos.'
Michael Carroll & Margaret Tholstrup [1]

I have a confession to make. I don't trust much of the literature on diversity in the supervisory space. Not because I am a diversity sceptic. Rather because it lets the supervisor off the hook too easily by reducing diversity to a few well-worn categories: gender, colour, ability, sexual orientation etc.. Yes to all of the above but let's not kid ourselves that our practice is diversity informed just because we have made small mental or operational adaptations to how we supervise or because we have a rainbow flag or a Black Lives Matter poster on our wall. It is one thing for me as a white man to cite black feminist theory, quite another for me to convince you that you can come to supervision 'as you are'.

My conviction is that every relationship is cross-cultural and involves diversity. You are you and I am me. Obvious differences like skin colour or age or gender are easy to notice and accommodate. But what about the ways we process information and make meaning out of experience to say nothing of neurodiversity or non-binary identities.

One consequence of understanding supervision as fundamentally about hospitality is that each supervisee and each supervision group teaches the supervisor how to be with them. Thankfully there is no fully comprehensive encyclopedia of supervision with entries on 'how to supervise gay men' or 'how to supervise multi ethnic groups'. And if such books ever get into print they should be burned since they diminish the relationality of supervision in which parties teach each other how to be together.

Stage	*Internal conversation*	*Interpersonal conversation*
Fear	What do I fear from this person? What do I fear learning about myself? What might I be avoiding admitting to myself?	What do we have in common? What can we both say we too? What concerns do you have about me?
Wariness	What if I say the wrong thing? What if 'they' stereotype me? How open and honest can I be with them?	How can we be more open with each other? What would hinder us from valuing each other?
Tolerance	What are my judgments about this person and on what basis? What boundaries am I seeking/applying with this person?	How can we exist side by side without friction? How can we remove blame from our interactions?
Acceptance	Can I accept this person for who they are? Can I accept them/their perspective as different from me?	What matters to you? What are your values? How can we collaborate together?
Appreciation	What do I appreciate in this person? How do they enlarge and enrich the world?	What can we appreciate in each other? How can we enlarge and enrich each other's worlds?

Table 2 Diversity Awareness Ladder adapted from Clutterbuck[2]

As a supervisee I was supervised for a time by peers who looked like me, were of a similar age, background and schooling but who completely failed to tolerate faith in the conversation. That experience was one of exclusion and a wounding failure of diversity. I also supervised a group of people training to become priests. When I pointed out the gender imbalance represented in the group of one woman and seven men I was attacked by the woman equally ferociously as by the men since 'gender is irrelevant, we are all just ordinands'.

As a way of raising the low bar set in the supervisory literature, David Clutterbuck offers 'The Diversity Awareness Ladder' (Table 2 above) as a reflective tool for conversations that supervisors or group supervisees might engage in.

Keeping it simple

When it comes to difference and diversity don't indulge in off the shelf lazy thinking. Every relationship is an encounter with difference. Every group is an encounter with diversity. Don't settle for diversity training. Treat every supervisee as your teacher and enjoy the learning.

Beyond what we see

Encountering another in supervision
is like entering a many chambered building
finding a way from room to room
through doorways and openings
meandering through hall ways
discovering stair wells
lingering in some places
quickly passing through others.
There are always discoveries to be made
and depths to be plumbed
Getting beyond the periphery
requires gracious invitation
to a gradual unveiling
of what lies beyond the threshold
And, as differences are revealed in a space
in which mutuality is acknowledged
there is honouring of the other
and the hosting of diversity.

Note 11 An Overview of Group Supervision

'Things should be kept as simple as possible but no simpler.'
Albert Einstein

In Note 1, 'Supervision in a nutshell' we established that supervision is a work-based, facilitated conversation involving a person's soul, role and context: a conversation characterised by the verbs connect, reflect, respond. That description still holds whether there are two or twenty people in the room. This is worth remembering especially when starting out as a group supervisor. At that highly formative time, many supervisors throw the baby out with the bath water, forget to connect, reflect and respond and tie themselves in knots worrying about group dynamics and behaviours. Given that supervisors have family history, it is not surprising that engaging in group supervision training can be unsettling for even the experienced one-on-one supervisor. Training in a group context may trigger old ghosts. Those whose histories lead them to expect groups to 'repeat' old family patterns may find themselves unsettled as survival takes precedence over learning. Those from secure backgrounds or who have worked hard at repairing their original family scripts may be disappointed by the lack of 'peers' they find. Whatever the entry point, novice supervisors may find the literature of group supervision intensifies rather than calms their anxieties. Thus for example:

> *'Group supervision has a lot to offer, provided that the supervisor has the competence to handle the dynamics in a small group and to understand the impact of organizational structures. Supervision in a group can never be seen as an isolated phenomenon. It is always part of a context defined by the surrounding organizational structure. ... Group supervision also seems to diminish hierarchical issues between supervisor and supervisee, increase the variety of behavioural and experiential supervision strategies, and help alleviate novices' perceptions of intellectual and emotional isolation.'*[1]

While I do not refute such claims, I would advise trainees not to start here. In my experience, an over emphasis on group dynamics, organizational structures and power differentials at the onset of group supervision training are likely to intensify professional isolation, rob practitioners of the little confidence they have and narrow their repertoire of supervisory strategies. When it comes to group supervision I am with Einstein: 'things should be kept as simple as possible but no simpler.'[2] In the hope of encouraging beginning group supervisors I offer the following guidelines all of which will be spelled out in more detail in later notes.

Guidelines for those who are beginning to supervise in groups

Clarity of Purpose

Group supervision has exactly the same purpose as individual supervision i.e. to foster an intentional conversation between soul, role and context. Beware of being so distracted or dazzled by the group that you abdicate your core purpose.[3]

Clarity of Role

The role of the group supervisor is to do exactly what the individual supervisor does ie to facilitate reflection. Beware of inviting reports. Beware of playing the referee. Beware of keeping everything cosy. Your role is to facilitate reflection. Abdication from that role is not an option.[4]

Clarity of Expectation

Everything that pertains to establishing shared understanding in individual supervision also pertains to group supervision. So be clear what the space is and is not for. Be clear about how the time will be used, which modalities may be employed, what the boundaries are.[5]

Handling Group Dynamics

Since groups carry echoes of family of origin, group dynamics are more likely to be about participants pasts than about anything you are doing in the present. Your job is to notice dynamics. Avoid being recruited into walk on parts in other people's unresolved histories.[6]

Family echoes

If you are picking up ambivalence within a group then bear in mind that groups may simultaneously provoke the desire to belong and the fear of being overwhelmed. Remember too that the twin dynamics of repeat and repair and their multiple variations may be at work.[7]

Search for Allies

To protect against overwhelm, group participants often unconsciously look for someone in the group who is like them (pairing) as well as for people who are not a bit like them (differentiation).[8] Secure participants value both likeness and difference. Less secure participants may value pairing over differentiation.

From I to We

Groups become groups when they are able to transition from *I* to *We*. If you want groups to be effective, spend time finding a value that the group holds in common and can say *We* to. A disparate nursing team becomes a group when it is able to say we want to offer our patients dignity and compassion. The '*We*' you facilitate will be invaluable in group cohesion and interaction.[9]

Take a long-term view of the group's life.

Don't hold the group to any one session. Multiple factors (conscious and unconscious; internal and external to the group's life) will impact on the quality of the group's life, experience and reflection.[10]

Prepare and listen to yourself.

Enter the room prepared and present to yourself and then attend to what happens within you as the session proceeds. You are there to facilitate the group to reflect. If you are truly present then your own stirrings are likely to offer information about group process and dynamics.[11]

Keep it Simple

As a supervisor know who you are. Know whose you are during sessions. Know whose needs you want to serve.

Supervisory Leakage

A space filled with grace
so pervasive
that one can't help
but bump into it
and the resultant spillage
illuminates
and transforms
encounter
A space filled with light
that seeps into
every nook and cranny
that rests
in dark crevices
unfurling itself
like a cat stretc.hing in the sun
until a different hue is detected

inviting fresh exploration
beyond the shadows
A space filled with presence
when souls show up
prepared for encounter
accompanying one another
beyond that which is visible in the room
tapping into a wisdom
that was waiting patiently to emerge
The hospitality of grace, light and presence
weave together in soulful encounter
when groups risk the vulnerability
of showing up and being seen.

Note 12 Attuning to the Needs of Group Members

'When it comes to supervision, hospitality trumps everything.'
Michael Paterson

If supervision is about hospitality then serving guests according to what they can digest is imperative. Here the seminal work of Stoltenberg and Delworth on the stages of supervisees' development is illuminative.

Originally devised in 1987 to describe levels of practitioner competence it has been reworked by McNeill (2010) and Hawkins and McMahon (2020) to suggest supervisory strategies.[1] I like to think of the supervisor as akin to a good host who would not serve her vegetarian guests meat nor her vegan guests dairy produce. In like manner, the hospitable host takes the trouble to learn what is nourishing for her supervisees, what leaves them hungry and what leaves them bloated.

The purpose of tabling stages in practitioner growth and development is not to pigeon-hole supervisees, to pre-determine their abilities nor to infantilise them by playing the 'supervisor knows best' card. The intention, rather, is to offer forms of bespoke hospitality which honour individuality and support insight according to each supervisee's abilities. As such attunement in supervision attends to three areas: levels of motivation and inner drive, self-awareness and the capacity to relate to others, and practitioner autonomy.

Supervisors in Training	*'Help me survive'*	
Cues & Characteristics	*Needs a supervisor who*	*Supervisors beware*
High in motivation, anxiety & dependence 'Tell me what is going on' (*Diagnose for me*) 'Tell me what to do' (*Prescribe for me*) ... 'Help me survive my practice!' Spotlight is on the Supervisor Supervisee experiences the supervisor as an expert practitioner, hangs on every word and takes copious notes Seeks someone who can help them survive rather than drown in the work they do	Knows the context in which the supervisee is working Welcomes expression of anxieties Is willing to be supportive and prescriptive Can focus on skills development broaden supervisee's repertoire of interventions build up the supervisee's confidence and self-belief.	Beware of being set up on a pedestal until discarded to the waste bin Offering remote therapy/care Issues of power imbalance Abdication of responsibility by the supervisee on to you Supervisor needs to monitor dependence & compliance in favour of building up supervisee's professional autonomy

Table 3 Supervisors in Training

Entry level supervisees are novices with limited training or experience and needing high levels of supervisory support and reassurance. In response they need supervisors who are confident in their abilities and who can act as role-models while at the same time doing everything they can to foster the supervisees autonomy.

Early days in any walk of life, whether that's starting out as a youth worker or volunteering for the Samaritans is a time of excitement. Investment is high. People want to be the best they can be. Nervous energy is often also high. This is the phase of professional sweating. 'What if ...? Will I be able to ...? I hope I won't mess up.' 'Help me survive says the novice. Don't let me crash and burn.' 'I'm here' says the supervisor, 'you can lean on me for now. I won't let you fall.'

Apprentice Supervisors		*'I could do with your help'*
Cues & Characteristics	*Needs a supervisor who*	*Supervisors beware*
Fluctuating confidence, and motivation 'How can you help *me* help the person that *I* am working with?' Spotlight is on the client/absent other Supervisee is *beginning* to find their way & express *themselves* as opposed to mimic the supervisor in the work. Spotlight, *occasionally* moves to an individual or specific encounter but when supervisee becomes anxious it reverts back to the supervisor again.	Either works in the same/related profession or has broad professional experience / repertoire of interventions, strategies etc Can help get detailed work into the room tolerate difference and allow supervisee to find own voice work with personal issues arising from the work in so far as they impact on the ability to do that work	Supervisors working with apprentice practitioners need to Track, monitor and affirm acts of independent practitioner activity (interventions, skills repertoire, clinical wisdom etc) in order to foster the supervisee's autonomy be patient with and contain the practitioner's oscillation between independence and needing reassurance

Table 4 Apprentice Supervisors

Apprentice practitioners have fluctuating confidence, competence and courage. They warm to supervisors who trust them enough to get started and find their way while knowing they can come back when they feel lost or stuck.

A few months into the work apprentice supervisees are like children riding on bicycles with stabilisers attached. They want to ride freely but often look back for reassurance. Their road sense is still that of a learner but they fall off less often and appreciate some tender loving care when they do. They like their achievements to be noted and are open to developmentally appropriate guidance and coaching to ensure smoother journeys ahead.

Independent Supervisors		*'I've got this complex issue'*
Cues & Characteristics	*Needs a supervisor who*	*Supervisors Beware*
Generally secure, stable in motivation, clear in purpose 'Generally speaking I know my way around ... but I could do with teasing out some complexities about Y' Spotlight moves freely between client, supervisee, unconscious dynamics etc. Supervisee see their in its wider context No longer a case of simply *surviving* in practice but of being at home in it, finding and using their *own* voice and style Supervisee is still grateful to have the supervisor's support behind them but is generally able to trust themselves and their own decisions	The supervisor need not necessarily be personally familiar with the work context of the supervisee and may be working cross-professionally. Need someone they can consult about complex aspects of practice Can celebrate supervisee's independence and expertise attend to unconscious processes tolerate not knowing Is robust enough not to collude or avoid can challenge can attend to wider contextual and organisational issues	Supervisors working with independent practitioners need to Trust that the expert on the work is the worker Withstand needing to know too much detail or context Allow the supervisee to direct the supervision session to get their own needs met Be attentive to communication by impact within the supervisory room Be attentive to parallel process, somatic resonance, embodied awareness, stray thoughts, images, songs, smells etc

Table 5 Independent Supervisors

The independent supervisor, knows what she is about and gets on with the job. Self-doubt arises from time to time but is usually settled by returning to first principles. If novice and apprentice supervisors were akin to children riding a bike with stabilisers, independent supervisors have a good sense of internal balance and can be just at ease riding on defined cycle tracks as off grid using their own inner map and compass. They see supervision as a regular opportunity to regularly like to meet up with fellow riders to compare notes, explore routes and increase their agility. They are just as happy to ride solo as in groups and value supervisors who share their 'can do' attitude.

Senior Supervisors		*'I value checking in with a consultant'*
Cues & Characteristics	*Needs a supervisor who*	*Supervisors Beware*
High level of internally validated expertise and of ability to make intentional use of the self in the service of the absent other. 'I take full responsibility for my own professional practice. I keep myself abreast through regular reading, involvement in professional bodies, CPD etc and am looking for a colleague for ongoing consultative support'. Supervisee directs the spotlight wherever it is required. Supervisor acts as reviewer, critical friend.	May know little or indeed nothing of the professional discipline in which the supervisee practices ie can work cross-professionally.. Can be a colleague rather than an expert Is not threatened by an equal Can help explore subtleties, uncover blind spots, strengthen professional integration and identity Can tolerate the complexity of situations to which there are no easy answers	Supervisors need to remember that Senior practitioners have developed an internal self-supervisor which holds them in check, encourages them and acts as a guide. As a result most of their professional practice will be supervised out with the session called 'supervision'. Nevertheless since they are working at depth senior practitioners can still have their personal and professional confidence thrown. Collegial though the relationship is, this is not a cozy chat but a professional space which belongs to the other ie the supervisee.

Table 6 Senior Supervisors

The senior practitioner is a leader in their field. They not only know the work they do but are deeply respected for the insights, originality and contribution they make to the profession more widely. Supervision gives them an opportunity to imagine new futures and develop innovative ways of working. They really value supervisors who give them wings to fly and with whom they can be accountable

Keeping it simple

As a supervisor, I don't show up for me. I show up for you. Help me know how best to be with you. Help me attune. Let me know when I underestimate you. Let me know when I over stretc.h you. I won't always get it right but if we can be real with each other we can press restart at any point.

Matching up

Sometimes supervision demands that we
serve up in the dining room
using silverware and serving dishes
and properly matched china
Other times, we gather around the kitchen table
where everyone lends a hand and digs in
not minding the odd assortment of crockery
What matters is that we know the difference
and accommodate others in a way that clearly signals:
Here is a space in which you are met as you are
and invited to go beyond
the comfortable and familiar
on an unpredictable
journey of shared experience and discovery.

Note 13 Group Styles

'Group supervision suffers from being widely practiced but little understood.'
Holloway and Johnston [1]

When it comes to group supervision, questions of style often come down to a range of factors

- Who is commissioning the supervision?
- If agency provided what is its organizational purpose?
- If it is a voluntary arrangement between willing practitioners what occasions the groups emergence?
- What is the function of the group?
- Who has a stake in the group's functioning?
- What legislative or reporting needs does the group have to meet?

Brigid Proctor identified four different styles of supervision group:

- authoritative
- participative
- cooperative
- and peer-group supervision.[3]

The main difference between these four styles is the level of participation that is invited and expected from participants. Eric Berne further distinguished them by four prepositions: in, by, with and of a group.[4]

	Supervision for Novices	Supervision for Practitioners	Peer Supervision	Team Supervision
	Supervision **IN** a group	Supervision **BY** a group	Supervision **WITH** a group	Supervision **OF** a group
Style	Authoritative	Participative	Cooperative Participative	Authoritative or Cooperative or Participative
Leadership	Supervisor led	Supervisor led or shared leadership	Led by a peer or peers in turn	Team leader or external facilitator
Composition	New to practice	Those in practice	Peers	Team members
Relationships within group	Trainees together	Prior or previous relationships	Subject to prior and current relationships	Subject to team dynamics
Benefits	Access to Supervisor's expertise	Access to group's wisdom and views	Strong on personal power and autonomy	May benefit the organization more than participants
Challenges	Competition, performance anxiety Fear of being seen	Hierarchies of influence Longevity of practice	Collusion and avoidance Maintaining the supervisory focus	Tension between supervision and management issues

Table 7 Typology of Group Supervision[2]

***Authoritative Group* – *In* a group**

Most practitioners are likely to first encounter group supervision in the contexts of professional training. Within that setting, they take turns to present their emerging practice to a more experienced supervisor from whom they receive coaching, guidance and feedback. The *advantages* of authoritative supervision is the access trainees have to an expert practitioner. The *risks* are that supervision dissolves into voyeurism, exhibitionism or serial supervision as supervisee after supervisee present. Beddoe and Davys comment 'by remaining in the role of expert and treating the group supervision as a session in which each member receives individual guidance a group supervisor can inhibit the development of group cohesion with consequent impacts on trust and participation.'[5]

Participative Group – _By_ a group

As practitioners develop their own autonomy and supervisory voice, participative supervision comes into its own as different viewpoints and perceptions are actively sought and valued. Supervision by a group has the *advantage* of providing supervisees with access not only to the authoritative supervisor but to the range of experience of group members and through them. Participative groups offer a rich opportunity for ongoing learning and development. The *risks* are that given the vacancy in an 'expert' occupying the seat of authority, other self-appointed experts rise up and pull rank based either on seniority or on assumed skill.

Cooperative Groups – _With_ a group

Cooperative forms of supervision such as that in which peers engage harnesses the energies of participants in the service of those with whom they work (i.e. their respective absent others.) The *advantages* are that the group collaborates and cooperates in creating the process, ethos and investment that suits them best. The *risks* are that peers may collude with each other, avoid the tough challenges that supervision requires and prioritises the social relationship (with each other) over the responsibilities to those in their care.

Team Supervision – _Of_ a group

Team supervision is less clear cut than the other three types of group supervision. Some team supervision is more akin to authoritative supervision with the team leader or an agency appointed supervisor leading from the front. Others are more akin to peer supervision with group members taking it in turn to facilitate the reflective space. Others again operate as a group of skilled practitioners supervising each other in a collaborative and cooperative manner. Given the vagaries, the advantages and risks are harder to delineate since any of the factors listed above may be in operation at any given time. Letting yourself and your practice be seen by colleagues you will be having coffee with later today, perhaps one of whom is responsible for appraising your performance, or another may be a competitor for internal promotion adds further layers to dynamics which will have to be managed if team supervision is to move beyond a tick box exercise, information exchange or team briefing.

Keeping it simple

When it comes to styles of group supervision, preferences are natural. Supervisors will have theirs every bit as much as supervisees will have theirs. It takes professional discipline to facilitate according to the requirements of your paymasters rather than just do your own thing. Let bespoke forms of hospitality take precedence over 'this is how I do it'.

Group Prepositions

In, by, with, of
are prepositions that matter in Group Supervision
Understanding the prepositions
enables clarity of purpose and focus
on the task of reflection
Failing to attend to the prepositions
creates an unhelpful blur
where lines are crossed
and focus is lost
where no one is met
and everyone leaves confused
Take care to distinguish the parameters
of the group's prepositions
so that the stated purpose
of reflecting on the work together
may be articulated and honoured
in a flexible, hospitable space.

Note 14 The Tasks of Group Supervision

'The lens we look through will determine what we see.'
Renee Swope[1]

According to Francesca Inskipp and Brigid Proctor the three tasks of supervision are Normative, Formative and Restorative.[2]

The *Normative* task of supervision deals with managerial issues; quality control; competence; compliance and ethics as typified in managerial supervision. The Normative task is the dominant mode of line managers and those responsible for ensuring standards, fitness to practice, safeguarding and risk management.

The *Formative* task of supervision is geared towards the growth and professional development of the supervisee through offering guidance, coaching, skills sharing and resources. Formative supervision is the dominant mode when working with people who are new to a profession or when significant changes arise in their roles.

The *Restorative* task of supervision tends to the support needs of supervisees, it offers encouragement; support; feedback; the opportunity for discharging feelings and for recharging energies. Restorative supervision is well suited when working with supervisees with oscillating confidence and competence. Supervisors need to beware that in supporting the wellbeing of the supervisee they do not fail to attend to the needs of their clients. Supervision is indeed about wellbeing but of both parties: the carer (supervisee) and those cared for (the client).

A supervisor's task is to know which conversation to have with a particular supervisee and then be able to engage in that conversation when needed.[3]

Five seater sofa

In the years following the introduction of Inskipp and Proctor's three legged stool, various accretions have been suggested. I find it helpful to construe the tasks of supervision less as a stool that supervisors risk falling off and more as a five seater corner sofa on which they glide from one seat to another as needed. In my mind, the restorative seat is the middle seat, from here I can easily move to the normative and formative seats on the left and the performative and transformative seats on the right .

As the name suggests, the *Performative* task in supervision ensures that supervisees are actually getting the job done; are keeping up with day to day expectations; meeting required targets; collaborating with colleagues and are accountable. The performative task is often the default task of line managers, mentors and coaches but its importance cannot be underestimated by any supervisor.

And finally the *Transformative* task of supervision sees professional practice as an invaluable teacher and views disruptive experiences, the kinds of experiences supervisees bring to supervision as invitations to dig deeply in search of their inherent meanings. The transformative task of supervision is likely to appeal to experienced practitioners who are lifelong learners and whose curiosity remains alive despite their years of experience.

Keeping it simple

'Take a seat' says the supervisee to the supervisor. 'Which one?' asks the supervisor. 'The one which offers the best view of the issue I am bringing today and what I want by bringing it.' 'Ok', says the supervisor, 'I'll start here and move along if required.'

Group Task

Mutual learning occurs
when the supervisor is prepared
to move beyond their comfort zone
and facilitate a space
that attends to the group's agenda
Listening to the heartbeat
Making a home for the unconscious
Attending carefully to the unspoken
Democratising the process of soulful reflection
allowing each one present
to discover clarity of purpose
to make the reflexive turn[4]
in their shared task of reflective process
Mutual learning involves moving beyond the I to the we
in the work we bring to reflect on together.

III

Part Three Who? What? How?

Note 15 Who is Group Supervision For?

'Groups provide a microcosm of the social world, with all of the drama and energy that comes with putting a number of actors together in the same room. Group supervision affords a context for both modelling and affirming practice, and for generating the cornucopia of possibilities that arise from the process of multiple dialogues.'
David Paré[1]

Supervision in groups comes in various guises. Some groups arise from the free choice of practitioners who wish to benefit from collaboration. Some are enforced on less willing workers who are mandated to meet for reflective practice. Some groups are a combination of *want to* and *have to* participants. This note introduces the vagaries of different kinds of supervision and the concomitant responsibilities of the group supervisor.

Supervising Trainees

Most if not all supervisees in the helping professions will have been trained for working in those professions in group contexts. Groups are the medium in which most training happens, supervision included. Sometimes those groups are homogenous: all rookies at the same developmental stage. Increasingly as people embark on second careers or pursue specialisms within their primary spheres of work, training groups contain varied levels of experience and self-awareness. A trainee dance movement psychotherapist in her twenties who is in their first term of training will have very different needs from her colleague in her fifties who is adding body-based therapies to her already established career as a counsellor. As a consequence, those who supervise trainees can no longer presume entry level knowledge, skills and self-awareness across the training group. Everyone in the group may be a novice in their emerging field of practice but it would be naïve to think that everyone in the group is a novice or newcomer to supervision and reflection on practice.

One of the consequences of training in groups is that the supervision trainees receive is often provided by their trainers or by those on their approved lists. While this is understandable and has the benefit of enabling group learning to be embedded in practice, those who provide such supervision would do well to remember i) just how costly groups can be for some participants and ii) that some behaviours within the group may result from what supervisees imagine parental figures (such as trainers) want to see.

This is not only problematic for participants but also for training supervisors especially if supervision-in-training has an evaluative dimension. Supervisors can only assess what supervisees allow them to see. 'Bearing the intimacy of scrutiny'[2] adds to an already complex personal and interpersonal dynamic. All the more reason to offer boundaried hospitable space in which inherent power dynamics are named from the outset and not avoided.

Supervising those who are sent

One of the paradoxes of supervision is that having been the preserve of psychoanalytic psychotherapists a century ago it is now increasingly promoted across a wide range of professions and disciplines. In some organizations, group supervision is part and parcel of being an employee or recognised volunteer. In other cases, while stopping just short of being mandated, refusal to participate in group supervision would be professional suicide. Some organizations promote supervision because they know its inherent value. Others use it as a tick box to enhance their professional reputation or to simply meet the requirements of regulatory bodies. Others again operate a caste system with individual supervision provided for those higher up the food chain and group supervision for those lower down.

Supervising those who are sent presents the group supervisor with a cluster of considerations. How do you create connection with people who simply don't want to be there? How do you foster reflection among people who refuse to let you or their colleagues see their practice? And what hope have you of any response resulting from the session if the conversation stays at surface level and never takes a deep dive into practice?

> Just because you are training as a group supervisor does not mean that you have to accept any group you can get your hands on.

Yes you need the practice. But no, you do not owe it to the world to supervise those who do not want to be supervised. If you do, however, choose to supervise the reluctant, or find it a requirement of your role, then I strongly advocate that you begin your first session by eliciting participants feelings about having to be there.

You may not think of yourself as a person in authority, but by association, for the participants you may represent the public face of the manager or company for which they work. Flushing out what is simmering beneath the surface can be very cathartic and bring a level of honesty to counter the 'feigned' (or not so feigned) buy-in that you are picking up in the room.[3] If you dare, you can invite people to speak out how they feel about being in the mandated supervisory space. If you do then be ready for the compulsive helpers who will come to your rescue and for those who played the peacemaker in their families of origin to show their true colours. Be ready too for the brave who might answer your question in forthright and possibly colourful ways. Be ready too for those in the group who will find the question confronting and may respond with hostility.

One simple way to find out how people feel in a group is to use non-verbal techniques drawn from sociometry.[4] An example:

> Holding a large cord or piece of rope in your hand ask participants to gather in a circle. Pass the cord around until everyone is holding it. Then ask the group to place the cord on the floor in front of them

> in the shape of a circle.
>
> Invite people to look at the circle on the floor before them and to view it as a representation of the open space of the supervision session. Tell people that on the count of ten, they are invited to cross the threshold and step into the circle if they are willing to give the session a go. Then countdown with the group and see who does and who does not join.
>
> If everyone joins then welcome them and move on. If someone hesitates or remains outside then gently ask them what it would take to be able to join. Alternatively you might simply invite them to sit the session out and proceed with those who moved into the circle. Sometimes actions speak louder than words and stepping into the circle may be a very potent way of a group transitioning from 'I' to 'We'.

Supervising the Willing

It is not uncommon for practitioners to make use of both individual and group supervision. Some groups are comprised of participants who first met in training, formed a bond and have chosen to continue together well after qualifying.

In other groups, practitioners have chosen to work together on specific areas of work in which the breadth of insights generated in groups are exactly what they are looking for.

Sometimes groups come together explicitly because of the wider range of modalities possible in a group, modalities drawn for example from playback theatre, or role work or systemic constellations. Working with a group of willing practitioners may seem easy but

> beware of equating a willingness to be in a supervision group for a shared understanding of *why* we are here, *what* we will do and *how* we will do it.

Whether working with those who *have* to or those who *want* to, it still falls to you as supervisor to check assumptions and establish group agreements. Five supervisors in a room may well have five different understandings of supervision, five preferred modalities and at least five sets of interpersonal dynamics. One person may be seeking reassurance. Another challenge. Yet another systemic disentangling.

As always the key to every supervision session lies in asking that two part question: 'what are you bringing *and* what do you hope to find by bringing it'. And while it is true that those who are steeped in supervisory practice may appear to self supervise, don't be fooled, such people often need the group's supportive and sustaining presence to do so and your holding of the group makes that possible.

Keeping it simple

Supervision is not mass produced nor off the peg but bespoke and individually tailored by artisans who are agile enough to effectively connect with the willing, the reluctant and the undecided. Know who you have in the room, what brings them here and then flex accordingly.

Who is group supervision for?

For the sent and the inquisitive
the keen and the reluctant
the assured and the tentative
the novice and the experienced
the expectant and the weary
brought together
shaken and stirred
a refreshing cocktail
when all agree to remain curious
about the process of group reflection.

Note 16 What issues do participants bring?

'The overall aim of professional supervision
is to develop the competence, creativity, confidence and compassion o
f the participants with ultimate benefits for patient care as a result.'
Mick O'Keeffe & James Forrest[1]

We established in the opening pages of this book that supervision is the name given to a facilitated and intentional dialogue between soul (motivation), role (post) and context (everyday realities, dynamics and people). As such it offers an opportunity to connect, to reflect and to respond in the work place. Generally speaking those who engage in group supervision bring work-based material which falls into one of four broad categories.

> Personal, Professional, Political, Prophetic issues.[2]

Personal issues

Supervision engages with personal issues, not through a therapeutic lens, but in so far as they impact on a person's ability to fulfil their role and responsibilities at work. Someone whose mind is taken up worrying about the mental ill health of their child will naturally find it hard to switch off those worries at work. Supervision can play a part in helping someone determine whether they are well enough to stay at work or whether they need to be encouraged to take some compassionate or sick leave. Similarly after a bereavement, supervision can be a good place to air whether coming back to work is what will provide the routine and structure to help someone 'get through' or whether they need to be advised - in their own interests and in the best interests of those they serve at work - to take time out.

Professional issues

The exploration of professional issues plays a major role in supervision. Having the chance to consult others about aspects of practice is the bread and butter of supervision. 'I found myself doing x and upon reflection wonder if that was the best course of action'; 'I have been invited to do y and am feeling in two minds about it.' 'Something happened at work which I just need to get off my chest'. 'A potential safeguarding issue has arisen at work which I would really value chewing over with you.' Supervision reflects on the past, in the present for the sake of the future. Each time zone is relevant but varies on any given day. Sometimes supervisees want to revisit actions, events, behaviours from the recent past of work. Sometimes they need to rebalance, recover lost confidence, or reconnect with their soulful purpose within the supportive ambience and unhurried space in the present. And sometimes their focus is on the future. Whatever they choose to bring, supervisees set the agenda. Supervisors harness the group's energies and follow.

Political issues

Supervisees sometimes value the chance to explore with their colleagues issues that might be termed political. Some examples: 'It breaks my heart that I am only allowed to offer clients six sessions of counselling and then have to discharge them' may invite reflection on the influence of the wider context in which the work is set.

'Under the new management it feels like we are being asked to do more and more with less and less resources' could lead to reflecting on organizational culture and ethos.

'I thought my job was about people work, but it seems all they care about is paperwork' could lead to reflection on statutory requirements and regulatory compliance.

In each of these examples the supervisor will have to be mindful not to allow the material one person has brought to open up a 'me too' bitch and moan fest or, just as inappropriately, a seminar style discussion of a topic. When political issues are raised in supervision the reflective question to the presenting supervisee remains the same: What happens to your soul when X is required of you in your role and context?'

Prophetic issues

No matter the age and stage of practitioners, soulful supervision can offer rich opportunities for exploring prophetic issues: dreams, longings and aspirations for the work or for the kind of practitioners supervisees wish to be in the future. Sometimes that future is as imminent as the next shift: 'Something happened at work today which I want to address when I am back there tomorrow.' Sometimes the prophetic dimension is well into the future as in 'I can't see myself doing this in ten years but its all I am trained for and that leaves me with dread'. And sometimes it takes the form of unfulfilled yearnings: 'You know if I could start all over again with the team I manage I would.' Speaking of prophetic issues in supervision Michael Carroll asks

> 'What if we could sit at the feet of the emerging future rather than at the feet of the frozen past?'

He continues:

> 'learning from the past is helpful when the past is a good guide to the future. But it leaves us blind to profound shifts when whole new forces shaping change arise'.[3]

Various factors will determine the extent to which issues of a personal, professional, political or prophetic nature are brought to supervision. Factors such as the *composition* of the group (is it voluntary or mandatory); the *developmental stages* of its participants (are they beginners, novices, independent practitioners or a mix of all three); the *style* of supervision on offer (is it authoritative, participative or collaborative); the requirements of stakeholders (is external reporting required; does group supervision play a part in professional registration or accreditation?).

More basic still will be the quality of trust and openness that exists between group participants. Supervisees who experience the group as out to get them are hardly likely to share their professional dreams and aspirations with the group. Conversely supervisees who feel held and supported may well be willing to trust the group with aspects of practice which do not show them at their best.

> Whatever the dynamics, supervision remains 'highly context specific and context sensitive' i.e. it does not deal in generalities or hypothetical situations or broad brush topics more suited to seminars but in edgy realities that stop practitioners in their tracks and cause them to ponder.[4]

There is a value in having a professional development session on complex bereavement with one's colleagues but that is a completely different thing from one of your colleagues exploring – in supervision – the ways in which they have become entangled in the complex bereavement issues of one of the people they support.

To ensure that supervision remains specific and not generic, supervisors need to pay attention to the verbs they use: reflect, explore, inquire all suggest honing in on something specific. Supervisory hygiene requires discarding the verb 'discuss' as in asking a group 'what would you like to *discuss* today?' Much better to ask 'what would you like to *explore* today?' Similarly I would advise against asking supervisees 'can you give an *update* on your work' and instead ask 'what from your work requires *reflection* today?'

> The stories supervisees bring to supervision are not the material.
> The stories are the bearers of the material.

Asking supervisees what they are bringing to supervision gets us half way into the reflective process. Asking them what they are hoping to find by reflecting, helps them distil the story down to its core and elicits what it is they wish the group to focus in on.

> What are you bringing for reflection today? What do you hope for by bringing it? How would you like to explore it in this group?

Picking up on the example earlier:

Supervisor: 'What would you like to reflect on today?' Supervisee: 'I feel like I have become entangled in the complex bereavement issues of one of my patients and would like the group's help to sort out the various threads and dynamics in the story.'

A further question about ways of exploring the material can ensure that the supervisee is helped to process complexity in illuminating ways.

Supervisor 'And how would you like us (the supervision group) to help you sort out those threads and dynamics.' Supervisee: 'I don't really know but am willing to trust the group'.

Supervision works best when supervisees have an investment in the issues they bring. Without that investment sessions are likely to feel flat and lifeless. Asking supervisees to name their intention for the session – their best hopes – has the capacity to engage both the 'presenter' and the rest of the group. Asking them how they would like to explore the material invites supervisees to direct the session while being held and appropriately contained by the supervisor.

As group participants become more familiar with the repertoire of supervisory modalities they may explicitly ask to explore their issues in a particular way. Sometimes the dynamics in the work-based material robs them of creative imagination and they simply want to be led by the supervisor. Secure supervisors might simply ask the group for suggestions as to how to proceed.

Supervisory modalities boil down to two broad categories. 'Tell me' and 'Show me.' 'Tell me' modalities include case presentation, narration, verbal snapshots, Inner Wise Guide[5], use of metaphor, Clean Language[6] etc..

'Show me' modalities include embodiment, visual representation, creative installations, use of art, percussion and music etc.. *Pastoral Supervision: Creativity in Action* (2021) outlines a wide range of modalities drawn from language, bodywork, drama, music and art which may be employed in exploring supervisory material.

Keeping it simple

Supervisees set the agenda for supervision. They determine what aspect of their work needs attention on any given day. Supervisors, like good hosts, then negotiate ways of working with the material that might yield best results. Don't be tricked. Language can be as creative as any other supervisory modality. Reporting isn't.

Up close and personal

There is nothing generic about supervision
nothing superficial
It should come with a warning:
"Deep work in progress"
Valuing others' time and participation
Honouring those they serve
insists that when practitioners gather to reflect
then work is front and centre
and practitioners are held securely
even and especially as they bump up against
hopes and dreams that are both personal and professional
or reflect on the practices they would like to challenge and change
or grapple with a context that seeks to silence or curtail
All of these find a home in the discomforting expanse
in which the personal, professional,political and prophetic
are offered and laid bare
for creative exploration in community.
That is the arena of Group Supervision.

Note 17 How many people make a group?

'One person is alone. Two people are a pair.
When it gets to three, there is a big leap in perception.
Within the three, there is a greater sense of cohesion and collective power.
If another person joins them, there is a further improvement.'
Changing Minds[1]

Issues of group size are based on a whole range of factors: time, developmental stage and supervisory modalities.

Time

In professions which view supervision as providing a form of expert guidance, participants may only be allowed to record the time spent in supervision divided by the number of participants. Thus a session lasting 120 minutes with four participants might only allow each supervisee to log 30 minutes of supervision. To my mind, this kind of thinking which arises from unnamed assumptions about authoritative supervision *in* a group[2] misses the point that

> in a group setting, when one practitioner reflects, all reflect and when one practitioner is supervised, all are supervised.

On that premise I would argue that supervisees should log the whole two hours of supervisory time rather than resort to mathematical equations. The size/time equation is replete with assumptions which will never be challenged if practitioners acquiesce and keep logging percentages.

Conversely, the supervisor who ignores the constraints group members are under in satisfying professional registration or maintaining accreditation or authorised practice, is akin to the meat loving host ignoring the dietary requirements of vegetarian guests. At the end of the day, when it comes to supervision, hospitality trumps everything and if that means groups have to be smaller or sessions longer to accommodate more numbers because of what can and cannot be recorded as supervision hours then so be it.

Developmental Stage

In the early initiation stages of any trade, trainees value being in groups which are both small enough to allow them access to the designated supervisor yet large enough to divert the spotlight of attention away from their shaky practice. In such groups the median size I suggest would be between four and six participants. Three invites triangulation. Even four is risky since one absence raises the same stakes. As confidence grows, and practitioners fixate less on 'me and my cases' they grow in their ability to learn from 'any case' that is presented. At this stage larger groups may be tolerated as long as there is wiggle room for emergency consultation and mop up within sessions. In groups of experienced practitioners, size will be less important than quality of interaction. As Steve Page and Val Wosket write 'the supervision issues of mature, experienced practitioners are also their life issues.'[3] On that basis they see themselves as the case that they take to supervision and the more insights they can access on that, the better.

Supervisory Modalities

I have often heard supervisors say that they are too busy to introduce creative modalities into their practice. What I understand them to be saying is this: 'There are four supervisees to get through in two hours. Its already pushing it to fit each person's cases into the 30 minutes allotted them. Adding creative interaction will inevitably mean we will run out of time and someone won't get their slot.'

Underpinning that kind of thinking is the mistaken belief that the more thorough the supervisor's understanding of the material the supervisee brings, the more useful they will be. Nancy Kline likens such 'listening to understand' to rearranging the furniture in the living room. The supervisee works hard in ensuring that the supervisor knows the story in such detail that they run the risk of boring themselves senseless by using all the air time telling the supervisor what happened where, when and how and then leaves the session with no new insight, curiosity or discovery. The shorter the time frame and the more participants there are, the less the supervisor needs to know. The supervisee knows the story. The supervisor's role is to help the supervisee access the wisdom they have but which is temporarily just out of reach. If it were not, why else would they be in supervision? Working from that premise, supervision groups can be very large indeed.

Keeping it simple

Before deciding on group size, critically assess your assumptions. While it is certainly true that everyone needs to reflect, it is not true that everyone needs to present their material. The larger the group, the more useful creative methods - especially those which do not require time spent on narrating the story - may in fact be. If you are not convinced take the question to supervision or better still enroll in a creative supervision group and see what depth of work can be done without narration in ten minutes.[4]

What counts?

What if numbers truly didn't matter?
What if what counted
was the willingness, alongside others
to enter a spaciousness
in which vulnerability is embraced
as reflexivity is practiced
to enable mutual growth
for the sake of those we serve?

Note 18 Benefits and Challenges of Group Supervision

'Our society fears difference. Google and Facebook have algorithms which steer us towards the like-minded, so we're tempted to live in bubbles of people who think the same thing.'
Timothy Radcliffe[1]

The most frequently cited benefits of group supervision are that is cheaper and saves time. It is therefore no surprise to know why group supervision may appeal to managers and to those who hold the purse strings. But ask supervisees about their experience in well-functioning groups and watch the list of benefits lengthen.

Group supervision, for many of us, has been the singular most important learning and development space post initial training. In supervision we have experienced theory dropping down into practice; honed our abilities to detect unconscious processes (transference, countertransference, parallel process, projective identification) at work; widened our supervisory repertoire; learned to tolerate difference and found freedom from some of our less helpful family echoes which can be triggered in groups. Those whose experience of group supervision has been positive can say with Brigid Proctor that group supervision is 'more rounded, lets in more light and air, and is less at the mercy of powerful, unquestioned influences and narrowness of focus.'[2]

> Group supervision lets in more light and air.

More light helps us see more. More air helps us breathe more freely. Less narrowness opens a world of exploration and creative imagining. In group supervision we can think aloud, try things for size and experiment. Group members' combined experience and competence provides a 'broader frame of reference' and exposure to a greater variety of work-based situations.[3] Group supervision can also 'diminish hierarchical issues between supervisor and supervisee and help alleviate novices' perceptions of intellectual and emotional isolation.'[4]

Challenges of group supervision

The challenges of group supervision are equally manifold. As participant numbers expand outwards from the individual supervision dyad, so too does the possibility for competition and exhibitionism between participants. 'I have more clients than you'; 'My work is more interesting than yours', 'Look how competent I am'. 'In supervision groups, hidden, non-acknowledged and unspoken competition often tends to be the greatest threat.'[5] Those who are unable or simply unwilling to compete can resort to hiding or defensiveness both of which disable the supervisory process which is to 'connect, reflect and respond'.

One way of defending against differences in a group is for group members to feign buy in and settle for a false unity. 'Group think' is a good example: '*Everyone here thinks..'*; '*We all believe that..*' Usually such behaviours arise out of a mistaken belief that differences always lead to conflict. Helping a group dismantle that myth may be among the best contributions group supervisors ever make.[6]

In group supervision the kinds of unresolved family echoes we explored in Note 7 may be awakened from sleep. Some participants may fall into repeat mode. Others may do all they can to ensure repair. Simpler still, some participants may go to extraordinary lengths to try and belong even to a less than effective group while others will head off in the opposite direction and become aloof if at all present.

Even within well run groups where family of origin dynamics are explicitly acknowledged and every effort is made to create an environment conducive to learning, supervisees can be 'overwhelmed by uncensored intensity of responses [by others in the group] to their presentation of clinical material'. Witnessing the impact their material has on others in the group may have the effect of 'closing down the group process, as understandably, there [is] a reluctance to offend anyone or put themselves into the firing line by saying the 'wrong' thing.'[7] And when this happens the light goes, the air thickens and survival takes priority over reflexivity.

When group life becomes challenging, group members with limited self-awareness may close ranks and join forces in attacking the supervisor. After all 'good parenting' would have saved the group from the discomfort they are experiencing. . The distinction between feeling comfortable and being discomforted by dynamics arising in the supervisory group or arising from the material that is being explored may be too subtle for some supervisees to distinguish and may need to be teased out by the supervisor.

Often what lies behind discussing the pros and cons of individual and group supervision is either an unstated economic stance which favours groups or a false binary stance which cannot see beyond either/or. The good news is that either/or choices between individual or group supervision are neither necessary nor advisable. Both/and offer a richer resource pool from which supervises can draw.

In one aspect of a person's work they may feel like a complete novice and appreciate a period of one on one formative supervision but they are just as equally likely to be drawn to the encouragement that comes from sharing that space in a group with others who are also finding their feet. Likewise a person may appreciate the opportunity for consultative support that peer group supervision gives them or seek out a specialist to have that need met on an individual basis.

Keeping it simple

Almost every book on group supervision lists its advantages and disadvantages. But why rely on second-hand material? Invite your group to make a creative installation using whatever is to hand to represent the group from Heaven and the group from Hell and you will unearth invaluable information not only about advantages and disadvantages of groups but about what to watch out for in the group you are trying to supervise.

The power and potential of Groups

It's not just about soliciting different opinions
or considering different perspectives
Not even about harnessing collective wisdom
It's about following the ripples
that work their way across oceans
when a stone is dropped in a pond
Finding that thread
that takes us into territory
that we could never have imagined
by staying in our own echo chambers
The risk involved in straying beyond our usual confines
is outweighed by the vast potential of discovering
a whole new vista that leads
to the transformation of our practice.

Note 19 The Role of the Group Supervisor

'Work of a transforming nature needs trained and experienced guides.'
Sheila Ryan[1]

There are three demons which besiege the Group Supervisor: possession, mastery and control.[2] All three have voracious appetites. All three need to be tamed. All three distort.

Possession, the thinking that lies behind 'my' group distorts the truth that groups are works of co-creation. They belong collectively to those who participate in them, who nurture them who tend them and invest energies in them. Without participants there is no group for the supervisor to possess.

Mastery, the belief that the supervisor is the expert, has the wisdom the group needs or is so skilled that the group could not manage without them is equally distorted. Yes the supervisor has a role to play, and depending on the style of group[3] perhaps even a key one, but their role is to harness the group's wisdom not to dazzle participants with their supervisory prowess.

And *Control,* not a word many of us are willing to admit to and yet how easy it is to control rather than facilitate a group especially if the group is characterised by differentials of practitioner experience, different degrees of self-awareness or people from different rankings within an organization.

> Good supervisors monitor the amount of oxygen they use in the room.

Those who supervise groups need to be 'appropriately authoritative but not authoritarian.'[4] Supervisors have role authority - authority accorded them as hosts of reflexive conversations. Outside of the supervisory room, their authority may have been accorded them by professional accreditation bodies but once the door is closed and a supervision group is underway, their authority will have to be earned by their attitudes and behaviours.

Supervisors who have tamed their demons neither possess, master nor control groups. Rather they bring their expertise in facilitating reflexive conversations to groups which in turn bring their expertise as practitioners and co-supervisors. Aware of their role, effective supervisors temporarily lay aside their need to belong to the group (in the same way as group members) and realise their need to stand just a little outside of it. Merging with the group serves no one but neither will being a complete outsider. Supervisors need to learn the importance of differentiated belonging.

The Task Needs	Group supervision attends to
To facilitate a work-based conversation between Soul, Role and Context which results in action (response).	clarity of purpose the absent other(s) standards of practice
The Needs of the Group	**Group supervision attends to**
the need to foster an ethos conducive to learning which allows participants to Connect, Reflect and Respond.	group dynamics communication & collaboration enablement & empowerment
The Needs of each Individual.	**Group supervision attends to:**
each group member has their own needs, pressures and trigger points. They are also members of other groups (family, local work setting etc) with their own needs to fulfil.	support & encouragement catharsis & letting go energy & restoration

Table 8 Role of Group Supervisor

Three Needs within Groups

Based on his work with service personnel across the world, John Adair identified three needs that group leaders attend to. The *Task* need; the *Group* need and the needs of *Individuals* within the group.[5] A simple illustration:

If you run a biscuit factory then the task need is to make biscuits and to ensure that your biscuit remains a market leader and product of choice. But you won't be able to make biscuits unless you look after the needs of your staff. Treat them well and they will make biscuits. Treat them badly and they will walk out, strike, or be so obstructive that you risk getting anything more than the bare contractual minimum out of them.

But it is not just your staff as a whole that need to be considered but each individual employee. If Mary who has worked for you for years becomes arthritic and can't do what she used to do, you will have Union reps and angry colleagues at your door if you try to get rid of her because she is no longer of any use to you. On the other hand, if staff see that you take Mary's needs seriously, that you recognise her contribution and her loyalty to the company and redeploy her to duties she can manage, the chances are you will not only keep Mary's respect but also those of her colleagues.

Applying Adair's insights to group supervision, effective group supervisors need to attend to three things: the Task of group supervision, the Group of supervisees and the Individuals within the group. But herein lies the problem.

- What is the task of group supervision and what is its purpose?
- Is it education?
- Is it professional development?
- Is it group counselling?
- Is it a space for reflection or is it really about reporting?
- Is it about fostering practitioner autonomy or is it about governance?

The failure by supervisors to state in clear and unambiguous terms the purpose of group supervision is the single most common reason that group supervision never takes off. And without that clarity of purpose - why we are in the room and what we are here to do - the slippery slope begins.

In my experience, it can be a struggle to do justice to all three of the needs that John Adair identifies when supervising a group. At times I have lost sight of the supervisory task, have abdicated my role in fostering reflection and disappeared down the rabbit hole of offering personal support to one member of the group while everyone else watches or joins in. At times this has been to the group's relief since the longer I spent on an individual who was distressed, the less time there was for the rest of the group to show each other their messy practice. I have also seen the opposite when supervision group members begin to persecute one of their own for taking up so much time and attention and for making others feel left out and ignored.

Another variation on the failure to keep Task, Group and Individual needs in balance can happen when the group sabotages any chance of reflection by distracting the supervisor from his or her true role by demanding that she police interpersonal rivalries or referee destructive behaviours within the group itself.

But it is not only needy individuals or dysfunctional group interactions that can scupper the effectiveness of group supervision. A sole focus on the Task to the neglect of everything else can be equally damaging.

When I was training as a counsellor, I was obliged to show up for group supervision led by the course leader who was so intent on getting the task done that she carved up the time between the number of participants irrespective of whether we group members were open to reflecting in the first place or had any investment in pursuing insight. By the end of the session, each of us had had our twenty minutes, but the over-emphasis on the Task, to the neglect of the human and interpersonal factors in the room, meant that compliance took over and reflection was eclipsed.

If group supervision *only* attends to the Task in hand (the work that needs to be done) without *also* attending to the participants as individuals and as a group, it risks leaving participants feeling dispirited and undervalued.

If group supervision only attends to the dynamics of the Group it risks becoming either a cosy huddle or a space for moans and groans to the detriment of individual differences (so easily lost in collective identity) and the reflective work that needs doing (the task).

And if group supervision only attends to the individual needs of group participants it risks becoming something akin to personal therapy to the neglect of the absent others in the supervisees' care.

Keeping it simple

'Bend me, shape me, any way you want me' approaches to group supervision might - temporarily - make you everyone's friend but will destabilise the group and leave you internally conflicted. Step into your role and then from that clarity playfully engage with the task, the group and each individual.

Paying attention

The skill of reading the room
Noticing the engaged and the withdrawn
Sensing the energy expended and contained
Wondering about the quiet and the guarded
Concerned about the dismissed or overlooked
Offering a rest from narration
Allowing the unconscious to emerge
Gathering up resonances
Inviting realisation
Making real the potential
of spacious supervision for all
is achieved by inhabiting the role of supervisor
with clarity of purpose and intention
the still centre around which
a group is invited to connect and reflect.

Note 20 The Role of Group Supervisees

'Supervision is all about the three 'R's:
Relationship, Reflection, Responsibility.'
Allan Brown[1]

The role of supervisees is to relax, breathe, enjoy and draw maximum benefit from the spacious, permissive hospitality which they collectively co-create with their supervisors: the slowed down pace; the gift of unhurried time; the opportunity to delve into things that really matter and to reconnect with whatever life-giving source makes the mental, physical and emotional demands of their work worthwhile.

Conscious that the supervisory space is shared with others, group members approach it ready to give as well as to receive, to support as well as to be restored and to risk as well as to be challenged.

> Group supervision offers a safe haven to *all* participants, not just to the needy, the greedy and the self-absorbed.

Without a doubt the supervisor has a role to play in modelling spacious and permissive hospitality but so too does each member of the group. The rehearsal of roles spelt out in Note 32 should be carefully monitored lest group supervision offers relief to some at a cost to others.

Supervisees who have been properly inducted into their role as co-creators and co-facilitators of group space assist each other to overcome the binaries of repeating or repairing old group patterns. Lending themselves to each other through noticing and wondering, somatization and parallel process, role work and creative engagement they become collaborators and conspirators in each other's transformative journeys: journeys marked by authenticity rather than pretence, engaged participation rather than detached observation. Not every group will manage that to the same degree and even the very best of groups will only manage it some of the time. But let not reality be the enemy of possibility.

In addition to contributing values and behaviours which foster reflexive conversation, the role of each supervisee is to come to group sessions having already begun to identify what might be worth their and the group's attention. That could be an itch in their practice that needs a good scratching or a nugget of gold they have discovered about their role in context or something which is worth celebrating in good company. Effective supervisors will have a range of modalities for enabling supervisees to explore whatever they choose to bring but unless supervisees take their responsibility for bringing it there is little chance of anything super or visionary happening.

Sifting through what has happened at work since the group last met is an art form in itself. To alight on one issue for further exploration is to say no to a whole host of other eligible alternatives. The sobering truth for beginning supervisors is that 99% of practice goes unsupervised and even the 1% which is, is 50% presentation and 50% interpretation. Bearing that in mind is deeply liberating since supervision is much more interested in meaning making than in fact finding. CCTV cameras can show you what happened. Supervision can reveal why what happened matters.

In preparing for group supervision, the following guidelines may be helpful to supervisees.

Authenticity.

Come prepared to be as open and honest as you are able on any given day.

Compassion.

Your work involves care for others. Let supervision include an element of compassionate care for you.

Generosity.

Without neglecting your own needs, try as best you can to make yourself generously available to others in the group especially those who irritate or misunderstand you.

Reflection.

Irrespective of the group style or supervisory format, come to every session intending to explore at least one aspect of your practice. Even if the session is taken up with other peoples' issues, you may experience a shift in perspective if you keep that issue in mind.

Realism.

Levels of trust, of insight and of creativity will vary from group to group. Be realistic about your expectations for this group which may not be ideal.

Investment

Make sure you are invested in the issues you bring to the group for exploration. If not you risk wasting your and the group's time.

Play

Supervision does not have to be an ordeal. Relax. Breathe. Experiment. Play!

Keeping it simple

Supervision is all about relationship, reflection and responsibility. If the group isn't going well, check which of the three 'R's needs attention. If what is missing lies within yourself then have the courage to address it. If it lies with the group then call it out. Your naming it is an act of commitment to the group's life and future.

Becoming a Supervisee

She stopped at a passing place on the track
to look back and see
how far she had come
It seemed a long way
But the winding path
did not even begin to tell the story
of forays into the undergrowth
to examine what lay beneath
Or of stepping off the known pathway
to explore alternatives that held a different kind of potential
And it seemed that wisdom and growth was to be found
in the apparent diversions
rather than in the way the crow flies
Co-creating covenant made more sense along the way
than at the beginning
As she reviewed the journey, she discovered
how she had slowly become
as she stepped off the track
to take time to reflect.

Note 21 Structuring Group Time

'The real power of Jazz is that a group of people can come together and create improvised art and negotiate their agendas.'
Wynton Marsalis[1]

Sat Navs are navigational tools which ensure safe travel from A to B but they are no substitute for drivers' instinct and the ability to respond quickly to changing road conditions. The supervisory Sat Nav offers a route from beginning to end of a session which, in the hands of a skilled supervisor, can be adapted as required. The six processes apply equally to individual and to group supervision. [2]

Hosting and containing

The opening part of the supervisory session needs to be expansive enough to offer hospitality to all participants, the fearful and reluctant every bit as much as the confident and the eager. Preparing a welcoming environment for in-person gatherings or carefully selecting what online participants will be seeing of your space when working online are part of hosting and containing as is whatever you do to help people make the transition from what they were doing *before* the session to what they will be doing *during* the session. A carefully chosen piece of music, the reading of a poem or the screen sharing of a calming image can all be used to help that transition and to set the tone for time out from the busyness of the day.

Eliciting and Focusing

Having established an ethos conducive to reflection, the supervisor has two further tasks: i) to get work into the room; ii) to draw on the presenting supervisees investment in bringing the work for exploration. Some examples:

'Call to mind the work you have been doing since we last met, and choose an image card which resonates with where you are just now'. (Packs of printed cards are readily available for purchase but your own curated collection can work just as well.) If you are working online then you could send participants a pack of e-cards which they can keep on their desktop ready for use via screen sharing. Remember that getting work into the room (eliciting) is only half of the equation. Focusing requires the supervisor to ask supervisees what they are hoping for in bringing their work (represented in the image) to the group for reflection.

Six minute journaling is a time economic way of eliciting and focusing. Give the group an opening phrase eg. 'The thing about work right now is ...' and invite them to write or type for the next six minutes freestyle. When the time is up, invite group members to re-read what they have written and to highlight three or four keywords. Finally, ask people to give their issue a title. That process ensures that every member of the group will have reflected on their working lives even if only one or two go on to take their reflections further in group supervision that day.

Beginning group supervisors can be just as anxious about no-one offering to bring material for supervision as they are about too many people wanting to claim group space. Having given the material a title, the group could be invited to hear the titles without any further explanation and then vote on which to work with. 'If you were going to work with someone else's material today who would you vote for?' In-person groups could indicate their choice by moving to stand alongside the person whose title resonates with them. Online groups could indicate their choice by entering the name of the person into the chat facility.

Another way of finding out who wants to bring something for the group's reflections is to demarcate a hot and a cold end of the room in which the hot end of the room means 'I have a burning issue' and the cold end means 'nothing burning for me today'. Asking people to take a physical position within that clearly demarcated space affords participates choice and gets around issues of voting. If working online, the same exercise could be adapted using the fingers of one hand in which 5 means 'I am really keen' and 1 means 'I am not at all keen'. On a count of three people could indicate their choices.

Exploring and imagining

Having created a trusting atmosphere and gone on to identify what someone is looking for by bringing work-based material to the group, the third process 'Exploring and Imagining' requires the supervisor to match supervisory modalities (ways of working) to supervisory questions (what is presented).

Issues which are bipartisan 'on the one hand' but then 'on the other' lend themselves well to multiple chair work in which one chair or position in the room is designated for option one and another for option two. Inviting the supervisee to physically inhabit each space successively and to speak out of each option separately can go a long way to disentangling thoughts, feelings and actions.

Groups offer a rare opportunity for supervisees to try out new roles or ways of being in response to work-based situations and dynamics. Inviting group members to play the roles of key characters in the workplace, placing them in relation to each other within the space and experimenting with finding one's own voice in speaking to them can be deeply illuminating.

> Whatever modality is chosen to enable the material to be explored, group supervisors need to remember that group supervision is not one on one supervision with a passive and silent audience.

Bringing the group in as early as possible enables the multiplicity of voices and views to be heard. Two caveats to keep in mind: i) no matter how keen you are to bring the group in, do not do so until the presenting supervisee has made it clear what they are looking for and ii) beware of overwhelming the presenter with the group's whoosh of responses.

As a rule of thumb it is often best to simply ask the group to say what they notice or wonder about what they have heard or seen and then after a few contributions ask the presenting supervisee if anything that has been offered back to them resonates with them. If so, pursue it. If not, leave it and move on.

Tracking and Monitoring

Tracking and Monitoring runs throughout the whole session.

As the group gathers, the supervisor will be tracking who is here, how the group is interacting and noticing anything which may impede the reflective process.

As the group settles in for the task of supervision, the supervisor will be monitoring energies, levels of participation, dynamics arising etc..

Tracking continues in relation to time especially where time allocation has been promised to ensure fairness among participants.

Tracking the journey from issue presented to insight gained, from present situation to what will happen later is one of the supervisor's main responsibilities as is monitoring what ignites and what deadens the presenter and group members as the session unfolds.

Bridging and Enacting

If supervision reflects on the past in the present for the sake of the future, then bridging and enacting - identifying what will be taken back to the world of work from the reflective session - is what distinguishes supervision from simply letting off steam. In group supervision bridging and enacting occur in two ways. Firstly, the supervisor asks the presenting supervisee what they will take away from the time of reflection and then (having closed that pieces of work) invites group members to name what they will take back to their *own* practice from the reflection. This needs careful handling to prevent group members re-opening the presenter's story and either directly addressing the presenter or making unhelpful comparisons between themselves and the supervisee.

With the presenting supervisees' work clearly closed, bridging and enacting group invites group members to succinctly name any resonances for their *own* practice. 'I realise I have some assumptions to check'; 'I am going home to think about how I avoid things until they spill over' etc..

Remembering that bridging and enacting comes towards the end of the session, supervisors need to be mindful to invite simple take home statements which need no explanation nor need to be understood by anyone other than the group member who makes them. Supervision is not a forum for information exchange but for insight to be found. If someone in the group has found insight- even if the rest of the group has no clue what they are talking about - the supervisory task has been accomplished and we can move on.

Reviewing and Closing

Hospitality in supervision is seamless and is as much about ending well as it is about beginning well. Ensuring that group members are in a psychologically safe state to leave session is one of the supervisor's responsibilities. When the material that has been explored has been highly emotive or on occasions when the group dynamic has been fractious, supervisors might intentionally begin the review earlier than the last ten minutes or so of the session. Being clear about the date, time and venue for the next session is also part of safe containment and good session endings.

Sat Navs get us from A to B. In so far as they do that they are useful. But the real art is to gently guide a group through its own highways, byways and dead ends with as much grace and hospitality as you can muster.

Keeping it simple

'Are we there yet?' 'Depends where there is?' 'Didn't you set the Sat Nav at the beginning?' Deciding where you want to go and how you want to get there offers the best chance of arrival. Being ready to face road closures takes supervision to a whole new level.

Group Process

Finding ourselves
in another's story
Identifying resonance
in another's wisdom
A whole group
is enabled to engage in reflection
as they carefully hold space together
And as a session unfolds:
As hospitality is offered
and focus is elicited,
issues explored and imagined,
tracked and monitored,
and a bridge back into practice is identified,
each can review how,
in our purposeful meandering together,
we have enabled learning by our reflection.

Note 22 Supervising Teams

'Practitioners operate in silos, intervening behind closed doors, intermittently sharing truncated verbal accounts of their practice with over-extended supervisors more intent on managing risk than developing practice.'
David Paré [1]

The supervision of teams is worthy of particular consideration for a number of reasons.

1. As a style of group supervision it defies categorization since it can be authoritative, participative or indeed collaborative.
2. In terms of leadership, it can be led by the team leader, by a facilitator from outwith the team or by an external supervisor.
3. With regards to content, it runs the risk of prioritizing operational matters (team catch up; debriefing; planning and scheduling etc...) over reflective matters.
4. It intensifies the group dynamic since the team has an ongoing dynamic which both pre-dates supervision and outlives it.

At best, Team Supervision can allow 'the doors to be shut, the noise to be reduced and a quiet space for satisfying professional conversation.'[2] At worst, Team Supervision can allow voices to be raised, fingers to be pointed and blame apportioned. All the more reason then why Team Supervision needs to be meticulously negotiated between the various stakeholders:

> The stakeholders in team supervision are the *organization* the team *manager team members* the *supervisor.*

Each of those parties has an interest in the supervision that is offered and finding common agreement between them will require some negotiation.

Picking up on John Adair's work in Note 19, each of the stakeholders might offer differing responses to the question: 'What is the task need of Team Supervision?'

In a Social Work setting for example, the organization may be required by law to provide some form of supervision or reflective practice to its staff without which staff would lose their licence to operate.

The manager (who may or may not intend to participate in team supervision) may be more interested in compliance (in keeping her bosses happy) or be absolutely convinced of the importance of supervision and see it as an invaluable support for her work.

Members of the Team for whom supervision is provided may have a range of positive and less positive experiences of group reflection gained in previous employments.

And into all those dynamics arrives the supervisor wondering what on earth she can do with a group with oscillating levels of understanding, investment and commitment.

Within Team Supervision, the ongoing relationships that team members have with each other outside of supervision are also going to be present in the supervisory space. Some of those relationships will aid the reflective task. Some will impede it. Many of the advantages and disadvantages which are generic to group supervision and were explored in Note 18 will be manifest. So too will what Wilfrid Bion terms 'twinning' and 'pairing' as colleagues side with each other and open the door to collusion and avoidance.

> 'The twin dangers of collusion and avoidance are almost certain to threaten the efficacy of the work where the participants have a vested interest in maintaining a sound working or social alliance over the supervisory relationship.'[3]

Collusion in supervision is subtle. It can look like empathy. It may even be intended as empathy but it is often a form of misplaced loyalty. Taking a colleague's side, agreeing with her version of events or interpretation of what happened and what needs to happen next may seem like empathy but all it offers a team colleague is another version of herself rather than a view from outside herself with which she can critically engage.

One way of working with teams who have a shared context is to make use of supervisory modalities that do not require supervisees to disclose (in narrative form) what it is they are presenting.

For several years I was the external supervisor for three teams within a large organization. Over a few sessions I began to notice that my opening invitation, 'Who in the group has something they would like to reflect on today?' was met with stony silence and a heightened sense of interpersonal awkwardness. I decided to change tack and told the group that – as an experiment – we were going to work in a way that no one would be asked to disclose what the supervisory issue was.

'Using anything that is in the room, I invite you to create a visual installation that expresses how it is for you to be in this room with your work colleagues today.' The group then had ten minutes in silence to create their representations. For the first time in several months everyone became engaged, collecting items from around the room and taking themselves off into corners where they could have some private space. When the ten minutes was up I reminded people that no one would be asked to explain anything verbally. Instead I suggested that we use the three levels of seeing to say what we noticed or wondered about each installation: I then asked if anyone would like us to visit their installation and allow us to notice and wonder aloud with them without them having to explain or disclose anything in return.

One team member said she was willing. The group gathered around. 'I notice your jug is very small'; 'I wonder how many times a day you would have to fill that up'; 'I notice the cup next to it is four times its size'. (The supervisee in question told me afterwards that she had been reflecting on how inadequate she felt in her role and how much her confidence needed topping up.)

That work-based story was unlikely to be told in verbal narration. Using a non-disclosive supervisory modality she had not only been able to explore her issue, present it in ways which she found illuminating but had also -to her surprise - encountered the compassion and support of her colleagues with whom she had been at loggerheads. The risk I had taken in changing the supervisory approach to allow team supervision to take place had paid off. The maxim 'if you always do what you have always done, you will always find what you have always found' came to mind. It was not for me to change the team dynamic but it was for me to change my approach to enable supervision to happen in that team because of that dynamic.

Team supervision also has an important role to play in helping organizations deal with reverse parallel process i.e. the 'distress, disturbance, fragmentation and need' of those they seek to support. In simple terms, I think of reverse parallel process as organizational indigestion, those aspects of caring for others which are hard to swallow and which cause institutional reflux! Not surprisingly, those who work with the homeless may discover that they carry around within them parts of themselves which have no fixed abode, and which restlessly look to be homed and housed. Those who work in Emergency Care can find themselves viewing a picturesque rock face and automatically wondering how long it would take to get a stretc.her down there when someone jumps rather than enjoying the view. And those who work with disturbed children may well find the behaviours of the children played out within the staff team as they push the pain upwards to their managers and up further to Board level.

> *'Good team supervision increases the ability of the team to contain pressure, stress and disturbance. What the team does not contain can spill out into the department or organization. Communication channels are the first to suffer, with projections increasing, not only from the team on to management and other teams but also on to the team from other parts of the organization.'*

Without such care 'the team can become the scapegoat for the organization.'[4]

Team supervision can be deeply transformative but it takes real clarity of purpose together with hefty doses of professional courage not to get caught in collusive and avoidant behaviours which favour one set of stakeholders over another. Above all those who offer team supervision need to continuously monitor the dynamics they become embroiled in for which supervision on supervision will be invaluable.

Keeping it simple

The best and the worst of team dynamics will inevitably manifest in supervision and keep team members and supervisors on their toes. Inhabiting the role of reflexive host will save you from having to referee between warring parties or colluding with the self-satisfied. The good news is that supervision is still possible even when recounting the story isn't.

No words needed

Not all stories need words for the telling
Often sense-making is found
in projection
or embodiment
turning up the volume
on energies that resonate
at a frequency other than sound waves
An invitation to examine
feelings that run deep

without having to articulate or interpret
for the benefit of others
can be a lifeline
in a workspace
filled with words
a lifeline that taps into the unconscious
revealing truth
unearthing wisdom
fostering trust
encouraging commitment
to a communal endeavour
by which growth ensues.

Note 23 Peer Supervision

'Reflective practitioners have three characteristics: they are open-minded, responsible and wholehearted.'
John Dewey[1]

Over the years I have found peer supervision to be the hardest and most challenging form of group supervision for me personally. My peers have indeed been open-minded, responsible and wholehearted reflective practitioners. The problem has been with me. Like many in the caring profession I can easily give way to others especially when it would appear that their needs are greater or that what they are bringing to supervision has more urgency about it than what I am bringing.

Despite my best intentions and my colleagues best efforts to ensure equity by taking turns of who goes first, I have from time to time either changed the focus of what I had intended to look at or simply allowed the time to be used up by others. This has not been deliberate on my part. Nor would it be fair for this to be seen as simply diversionary or blatantly evasive. It has happened spontaneously. I arrive, share coffee and catch up in conversation during which someone discloses that they are having a hard time, or are working through personal issues or some other pressing variable. Before I know it, I give way and time and time again return home not having actively had my needs met in those sessions.

Having spoken with others, I find I am not alone in this. The vagaries of individual circumstances are present but something of our early family patterning kicks in almost in reverse.

> It begins with your family but soon it comes around to your soul.[2]

Those who spent their childhoods looking after parents or who stepped (prematurely) into the empty shoes of the responsible adult in the family system 'often forge a lifelong pattern of over extension'.[3] Paradoxically, in spaces where that pattern of being the carer does not require to be repeated (as is the case in peer supervision which advocates relationships of mutuality and equality) the default setting can easily kick in. Peers who spot unresolved family of origin dynamics in each other can offer an invaluable reparative experience. Peers whose own needs lead them to take care from anyone who will give it probably won't notice. Sheila Ryan's counsel is apposite here:

> 'In trying to supervise each other's *cases* instead of supervising each other we were missing a golden opportunity. It was *us* who were present in the room .. not the actual patient. Surely it was us who could benefit from supervision directly so that we could in turn respond with more freedom, energy and compassion in practice?'[4]

Among the traps that peer supervision can fall into Gaie Houston (1995) enumerates

- 'Competing to be the most potent' (my clients are harder to work with than yours; my practice is more demanding etc.);
- 'Ain't it awful' (let's all plummet into helplessness and make helplessness our common denominator);
- 'We are all so wonderful' (this becomes a kind of protection racket since if I only praise or affirm you then you will repay me in kind);
- 'Who is the best supervisor?' (since there is no named supervisor, participants can jockey for the position through attempting to be more insightful than each other);
- 'Hunt the client' (describes the process by which a group makes one of their members the weakest link whom they all try to fix).

To overcome the hurdles of repeat and repair, those who engage in peer supervision need to be extremely disciplined about how they contract together. Peer supervisees do not have to agree a one size fits all approach but they do need to find ways of including all members needs within the peer space. The common denominator does not need to be low but it must include negotiating how to accommodate different processing styles, ways of presenting, preferred exploratory modalities etc.. One person may want to tell the story. Another may wish to engage the group in embodied role work. Another may wish to work in silence with art materials with others present as witnesses. Differences do not need to be ironed out. Complexity is possible. Constantly giving way is not an option.

Keeping it simple

Peer supervision is deceptively complex. It gets round the costs and can democratise power games but if everyone is to have their needs met, it actually requires more explicit contracting than supervisor-led forms of supervision. Supervision requires more maturity and ability to work with difference than most practitioners imagine.

Sabotage

That place where one might expect to be met
with equanimity and care
may also be the place where one fights for survival
A place where all our instincts of care crowd in
and crowd out our ability to ask for what we need
Defaulting to that familiar place
of subverting our own needs
Giving up our claim on the space
to allow others more room
we leave without having done
the work we most needed to do.
Now there is something to take to supervision!

Note 24 Supervising Organizations

'Supervision can help an organization breathe and learn.'
Hawkins and Shohet [1]

The majority of supervisors in my network offer individual supervision. A few offer group supervision. Fewer still organizational supervision. I find this simultaneously unsurprising and yet disturbing. Unsurprising since many supervisors find it easier to work with individuals and so much more comforting and comfortable to see the rewards of their labours as they grow and develop.' But while I find it understandable I also find it disturbing that the supervision industry is neglecting our organizations, our businesses and our public institutions. Michael Carroll could not put it more starkly: 'Organizations need supervision – badly!'[2]

It is easy to chastise those in power, to berate political leaders or lament the state of the public sector. For years I provided supervision on an individual basis to health and social care workers in Scotland. Day after day I encountered people who had started out with fire in their bellies. Day after day I saw those fires dampened down. Initiative after shiny initiative was rolled out to address the malaise each with increasingly sparkly launch events and publicity campaigns. But still the brain and talent drain continued. Like many I felt too small to make a difference faced with the Goliath of a system in decay. And the more I sat with individual supervisees from those public organizations, the more uneasy I became.

Was it ethical to simply patch people up for one hour a month knowing that they were invariably returning to the source of repetitive moral and psychological injury? At times, I longed for the person I was with to stay on after the session to meet the person who was coming next in whom they would hear their story echoed and their experience validated . So strong was my conviction that peers would do better meeting each other rather than individually with me that I dreamt of simply serving them tea and having them meet with each other.

And that was how Values Based Reflective Practice came to be born as a form of organizational group supervision in which the fire in the belly could be reignited and vocational motivation reborn. The Scottish Government gave it their backing and it is now established across the English speaking world.[3] Its formula is simple and begins by using the M-A-P tool which stands for

> Motivation - Actual Practice - Potential Practice.

Gather staff. Ask them what brought then into the profession in the first place (motivation). Ask them to correlate their original motivation -'I wanted to offer compassion and dignity to patients' - to the last shift they had been on (actual practice) and then ask how motivation played out in that shift. Finally I ask participants how they would like their next shift to go (potential practice). Joining motivation with actual and potential practice has offered a very effective form of organizational supervision with significant results in terms of higher levels of job satisfaction, reduced absenteeism and improved patient outcomes.

> Values Based Reflective Practice is about the re-humanising of care through the recovery of personal and organizational soul.

If supervision is about the dialogue between soul, role and context then organizational supervision is about deeply incisive and inclusive conversations about the *soul* of organizations, their *role* in the world and the *contexts* in which they find themselves. Those questions which supervision ask of individuals, are just as valid when asked of organizations whose life-cycles are every bit as much characterised by seasons of orientation, disorientation and reorientation.[4]

In simple terms, organizations, like individuals, start off knowing who they are, what they are about, doing what they are meant to be doing (Orientation) until something unexpected happens, something shatters their sense of equilibrium and throws everything off balance (Disorientation). And when that happens, individuals and organizations have two choices: they can give in, accept defeat, abandon hope and make disorientation their new home or they can dust themselves down, sift through the debris, learn from the experience and face the future with greater clarity and renewed purpose (Reorientation). It is my conviction that supervisors have an invaluable role to play in helping organizations recover their soul and in so doing enable them to heal the divorce which so often exists between being human and being simply efficient.

> 'The Master's tools will never dismantle the master's house. They may allow us temporarily to beat him at his own game but they will never allow us to bring about genuine change.'[5]

Organizational supervision is not an add on, an extension or an annexe for those that like that kind of thing. Organizational supervision has the potential to be the foundation of corporate life not least because it is inherently subversive. Organizations are prone to be self-serving. The needs of the system are often prioritized over the needs of those they exist to serve. Organizational supervision engages in soul recovery by

- Reasserting that what we have in common is greater than what divides us.
- Inviting staff to work from their soul outwards, rather than to leave it at home.
- Believing that the future is not already proscribed by the past.
- Welcoming wisdom wherever it lies in the organization.

Keeping it simple

Serial supervision of individuals one after another can seem like an easier option. But is it always the ethical thing to do if people are simply being returned to sites of workplace injury? What would it take to draw people together and help them rediscover the soul of the organization and find their collective voice in speaking truth to power? Organizational supervision is challenging but the contribution it makes to an empowered workforce can be immeasurable.

Facilitating change

When we see patterns repeated
When we listen time and again
to similar stories of systemic wounding
How might we best honour those with whom we work
and, in turn, those with whom they work?
How might we, as well as providing attentive listening,
also provide some gentle challenge
In exploring soul and role, what light
might we shine on context
that would affirm agency
to collaborate in change?
The simplicity of holding space
that enables colleagues to hear one another
plays its part in bringing about change.

IV

Part Four Getting Underway

Note 25 Running a Taster Session

'Try before you buy. Try before you deny.'
Tik Tok

Given the mystery surrounding group supervision and the inherent propensity that groups can have in triggering 'family of origin' material, offering potential supervisees a 'try before you buy' taster session can help those who are curious to find out if this is for them.

To truly be a 'Taster', what happens in the session needs to be consistent in ethos, style and ways of working with what you intend to offer should a group be formed. Beware therefore of overselling in the Taster only to under deliver in subsequent sessions. Be aware too that supervision is not in the business of chasing novelty but of pursuing insight. You don't therefore need to be all singing all dancing. And if you are, then ask yourself what leads you to take up so much of the group's space and oxygen.

You will have your own ideas for a taster based on the style of group you intend to facilitate, the range of modalities you intend to employ and the levels of practitioner experience you wish to draw into your group. What follows is a generic stand-alone taster session that you might like to adapt for your own purposes.

Environment

Before the group arrives do whatever you can to create an ambience that suggests space. If the room is cluttered try covering at least some of it with coloured cloths. If the room has movable furniture try clearing as much of it to the edge of the room as possible. If you have no option but to meet in an office around a table, try positioning something that takes the eye away from the office environment and softens it: perhaps a vase of flowers or colourful image cards scattered around the table? Whatever the environment in which the group will meet, consciously do whatever you can to introduce an element of surprise and anticipation in participants as they arrive. When even the ugliest and most familiar meeting room *looks* different (flowers) *smells* different (coffee brewing) or *sounds* different (music playing) curiosity is piqued and reflective wondering has begun.

Who is here?

At the appointed time begin. Starting early or late suggests poor boundaries. Starting on time implies you mean business. Before presuming that everyone needs to do the predictable round of introducing themselves to each other, check your underlying assumptions. This is a Taster session. It is not the first session of a ongoing group. Some people will never come back. Think twice about what it is you hope to gain by time consuming personal introductions? As an alternative way of beginning you could invite the group to form a circle around a piece of rope or ribbon placed on the floor and then to indicate their willingness to give supervision a go by stepping into the circle inside the rope (see Note 15).

For a Taster session you don't need to spend precious time on long drawn out contracting. In most instances a mini contract such as 'can we agree that what is said here stays here and that we will treat each other with respect in this session' is usually about as much of a mini contract that you will need for a ninety minute to two hour taster. Having made such agreements, the bulk of the Taster time is now available for you to facilitate a supervision session as you mean to continue.

Supervision

One simple way of ensuring that everyone in the group receives something from the Taster session is to use the M-A-P exercise in which *M* is for Motivation, *A* is for Actual practice and *P* is for Potential practice (ses Note

24). Participants are invited to choose a card for each and then in small groups to simply show which card is which without explanation and to hear what their peers notice and wonder in response. As always, the purpose is not information exchange but the pursuit of insight. Once the presenter has heard the group's offerings, they can be invited to say what they realise from the exercise.

Closing

Gathering the whole group back together gives the supervisor a chance to very briefly say that 'supervision provides an opportunity to reflect on the past in the present for the sake of the future. Today we used cards. Once the actual group gets going we might use a variety of tools. If you are interested in joining the group there's a sign-up sheet or if a chat would help you decide you can contact me. But to help us close lets gather again around the outside edge of the coloured rope. And now that we are gathered let's turn outwards facing back to the world of work and think about what we are each taking away with us from our time together today. Once participants have named their take homes, simply close the session.

Keeping it simple

A Taster needs to whet the appetite rather than leave people with indigestion. Keeping it simple will be far more productive and offer participants a more realistic taste of what they can expect if they sign up afterwards than an 'all singing all dancing' display of your supervisory wares. Whet the appetite and leave people wanting more. That's what it says on the menu!

From sales pitch to reality

The ad promised high spec luxury and comfort
The test drive was a blur of shiny sophistication
But when it came down to signing up
it turned out the fun and the wizardry was extra
And that was a relief

There was enough to get to grips with
I wanted to become familiar with the basics
which were complex enough
before engaging with another level
that, for now, was a step too far
For my assent to be given
I needed assurance
that the terrain would not push me too far
into the unknown
until I was ready for the next level.

Note 26 First Meeting with the Group

'Coming together is a beginning,
staying together is progress,
working together is success.'
Henry Ford

This note assumes that supervisors have prepared both themselves (Note 27) and group members (Note 28) to know what to expect. It also presumes that the physical or online environment has been adapted to suggest space, wonder and curiosity (Note 25). From experience I would suggest that first sessions of groups which are intended to be ongoing are structured in the following order: Who? What? How?

Who is here in the room?

Since supervision is relational the first task is to enable connection with those who are there. This is always paramount in any kind of supervision, but remembering the echoes that groups can carry from early life, supervisors would do well to choose carefully how to help participants encounter one another within a new group. Asking people to introduce themselves in turn may be unbearable for the withdrawn and irresistible for the exhibitionist. As always think carefully about purpose. Are you seeking information exchange (in which case potted histories and CVs etc. may be appropriate) or are you seeking connection (in which case exercises which enable participants to connect with values or deeply held convictions may be more suitable). One very illuminative exercise for finding out who is in the room is suggested by John Prowell (1999) who invites group members to introduce themselves through their own cultural lens.

- What is your name?
- Who named you?
- Does your name have a meaning?
- In your family/family of choice or culture, how are names passed on?
- Have you changed your name for any reason?
- Does anyone else in your family/family of choice carry your name?

Prowell (1999) notes how participants using such a process

> *'may reveal spiritual or religious connections to their names ... and the story or processes of how their name/s emerged. As the supervisor, I offer some questions inviting fluid boundaries around containment and disclosure to facilitate the worker taking space if they would like to make public more of their identity and culture. More self-disclosure is not required, however, and here negotiating and hearing 'no' on the part of the supervisor is important.'*[1]

What do group members have in common?

One non-threatening way of finding out what group members have in common is to ask the group to stand and create a circle. Once gathered explain that you are going to step into the circle and say something about yourself and if others connect with what you have said then they too are invited to take a step in and join you. Beginning with easy matters such as 'I am wearing blue today', those wearing blue step in and join you in the inner circle. 'I came here by bus' and so on. As the group catches on, invite participants to take the lead.

'I don't know why we are playing this silly game' is as valid a contribution as any since it allows the group to laugh *and* identifies what the group holds in common. The point of the exercise is to intentionally discover some of the dynamics that are in the room. 'I find groups a bit daunting'; 'I don't always find my voice in groups'; 'I don't usually join groups' 'I'm a bit nervous and anxious to be meeting so any new people in his group' etc.. Without questioning any of what participants offer, you and the group are now privy to a whole lot more information about each other than a round of CV type self-introductions would have delivered.

How will we be together?

Establishing agreement for how group members wish to be together in the supervisory space requires some imagination lest we resort to consigning words to a flip chart page that we never intend to show or refer to again. Group agreements need life injected into them not air sucked out of them. They are the group version of pre-nuptial agreements which marry together best aspirations (we will accept each other unconditionally) with a healthy dose of realism (we will say sorry when we get it wrong). The group's purpose – to engage in reflexive conversation – is not up for grabs but the 'how' is. Vikki Reynolds writes:

> *'Early in the formation of the supervisory group, I construct a conversation that opens space for us to connect around what is at the heart of our work. The purpose of these questions, which frame the conversation, is to centre our supervisory relationships in dignity and respect: What do we need to understand in order to respect you, make space for you, and not transgress against you in our relationship? What do you hold sacred, close to your heart, that it would be useful and important for us to know? In a cautionary introduction to the exercise, I invite practitioners to consider both the cost of speaking of parts of themselves, and the cost of not speaking.'*[2]

In some groups the Nine Beats of the Beatitudes may form the basis of the group agreement (Note 38) or Louie Gardiner's Seven Principles for Group Ethos (Note 39). By whatever means you elicit the group agreement make sure it is meaningful to group participants (rather than just a tick box exercise) and make sure it is captured physically (for example in a photograph that is shared around the group). Time spent on a group agreement is time invested in making reflection possible.

One fun way of flushing out residual experiences from other groups that participants carry with them into this group is to invite them to create a visual installation of the group from hell and the group from heaven. By freely associating with a range of image cards, figurines, small world collections and random everyday things that are in the room the group will inevitably revisit (even if not out loud) what they carry into this group from previous groups.

Using noticing, wondering and realising, the group can be invited to explore what makes some groups heavenly and others hellish. Astute supervisors will learn a lot about group members and receive a lot of implicit direction as to how to conduct this particular group e.g. 'it was one of the few groups I have been in in which people gave me time to find my words and didn't rush me to speak when I wasn't ready'. The astute supervisor is given a good steer by such a comment. Similarly 'I quickly learned that whoever shouted loudest or cried most got noticed and the rest of us didn't'. Treating everything as information, those two comments alone which emerged from what appeared on the surface to be a fun exercise about groups from heaven and hell are worth their weight in gold to a supervisor getting to grips with a new group.

Keeping it simple

Spending time on *who* is here, *what* we are here to do and *how* we will go about doing it is time well spent. It reduces stress and builds security without which reflection cannot happen. It also offers the supervisor very valuable information about the group's composition, history and hopes.

Bridging the chasm

My idea of heaven
may be your idea of hell
Figuring out how we might stand in the gap, together
will involve each venturing closer to the other
in order to find common ground
Not so that we can be the same
but so that we can move beyond
what makes us different
to find a way
to work together.
As we each resolve to hold with respect
confidences shared
hopes and fears revealed
we create a container
that allows us to take risks
as we shine the reflective lens
on our practice
gaining insight from experience
and valuing the space
that enables mutual learning
through shared reflection.

Note 27 Preparing to Meet a Group for the First Time

'How can I help is a timeless enquiry of the heart.
Without minimizing the external demands of helping others,
it seems fair to say that some of the factors that wear us down,
we have brought with us at the outset.'
Ram Dass and Paul Gorman[1]

Supervisors show up for their supervisees and not for themselves. The space they hold is for others not for self-validation. Making themselves intentionally available for others means that supervisors need high levels of self-awareness.

Before meeting a group for the first time, it may be helpful for new supervisors to reflect on the following questions.

About yourself

- If you want to know what is unresolved in your life, look at who and what you attract in your client portfolio. Part of the alchemy of supervision is that our supervisees often present with issues that we ourselves need to attend to.[2]
- Similarly if you want to know where life is nudging you forwards audit the kinds of issues people bring you (change management; dealing with trauma; vocational fulfilment; burnout etc.)

About your history with groups

- What assets and deficits do you carry from your own family of origin?
- What triggers unresolved issues for you?
- When triggered how do you re-balance, reboot and re-source yourself?

About the group you will be supervising

- What pre-transferences arise for you?
- What are your fantasies of what might happen?
- What do you sense about the group?

As you approach the first session

- What does hospitality for this group call out of you?
- What would support you to be available for the group's purpose?
- How will you boundary your own need for belonging and recognition?

After the first session

- Which of your fears were not realized?
- Where were the surprises in the experience?
- What did the group teach you about yourself, your role, the supervisory task?

Keeping it simple

Being self-aware allows me to show up for you without tripping over myself. It also prevents me using you to have my own needs met. It all comes down to role clarity and inner freedom. Being clear that I have come to facilitate a space in which others can connect, reflect and respond, I address anything within me that impedes my capacity to serve you. What I cannot resolve I take to supervision.

Before and after

Before I invite others to engage
I take time to examine what I bring with me
Can I own what is mine
while leaving room for those who will join me?
Will my self awareness
enable me to host a space
conducive to reflection
in which others can examine their hopes and fears
and feel met along the way?
And once our task is accomplished
can I be real about risk rewarded
or aspirations unmet
so that my learning informs
the way we work in the future?
Am I willing to do my work
so that I can enable you to do yours
as we share the space of reflexive hospitality?

Note 28 Preparing Supervisees for their First Session

'Group supervision is largely unchartered territory looking for pioneers.'
Allan Brown & Ian Bourne[1]

The best preparation you can offer those coming to group supervision – whether they are deeply familiar with it or complete novices – is a clear and unambiguous statement of purpose which says in your own words what supervision is and is not. Using your own words means you have to think in advance and not simply hope that participants will have a common understanding of what supervision is about. What Michael Carroll says of supervisory contracts is just as pertinent to pre-meeting expectations.

> *'Contracts are like icebergs with the formal, agreed and overt contract as the part of the iceberg that is above water, while the unseen, unnegotiated psychological contract is the part beneath water ... in our heads we work out an agreement with someone else ... unsuspectingly, we make them mentally sign it and thereafter it has all the force of a binding agreement ... it is often the difficulties in the psychological contract that results in ethical charges, formal and informal complaints, legal stances and breakdown in professional (and indeed personal) relationships.'*[2]

If we want supervision to get off to a good start rather than be marred by ragged edges then being clear, consistent and concise will be helpful. Here is a sample pre-session statement that that you could tweak for your own particular context and either mail out to participants in advance or poston your website.

Introducing Group Supervision

1.*What is it and what happens?*

Supervision is an opportunity for workers to

- down tools
- press pause
- re-connect with their motivation
- and reflect on their work in a group setting.

The role of the supervisor is to ensure safety, facilitate reflection and to keep the group on track. The role of group members is to pool their professional wisdom in helping each other explore issues which arise in the workplace.

2.*Practicalities*

The group will meet on *(date)* from *(time)* in *(venue and address)* / Zoom link details.

To get there by public transport .... Parking *is/is not* available.

On the day please contact *(name)* on *(mobile phone number)* if you are delayed.

Fees (if applicable) and invoicing process.

Supervisory Material

- Clearly state any preparation that is expected from participants prior to the session.
- If you are requesting a verbatim how many copies should be brought?

- If you are inviting people to bring something with them be clear what it is (a stone; a family photograph; something they can use to introduce themselves).
- What can people expect to happen at the first meeting?
- Please come with an open mind and oodles of curiosity!

Keeping it simple

Clarity from the outset allows would be participants to know what to expect and then, to make informed choices about joining the group or not. Supervisors who can be trusted to do what they promised to do will be rewarded. Those who change the terms and conditions as they go along will inevitably have to deal with the fallout.

There be dragons

Hospitality involves
preparing participants as best we can
for what they might encounter
Mapping out the territory that is known
Fostering trust for the unpredictable
Naming expectations
Bringing them into the light
Being real about risk
and then accompanying those
who remain up for the challenge.

Note 29 Boundaries

'Together we will create brave space
because there is no such thing as a 'safe space'.
We exist in the real world.
We all carry scars and we have all caused wounds.'
Beth Strano

Supervision, like therapy, often claims to offer people a 'safe space'. And so it should. But safety is not the goal of supervision. Rather the goal of supervision is to ensure that awake, attentive and agile workers give their very best to those in their care. If safety in the supervision room contributes to that then all well and good. But if safety, or what passes as safety, becomes the end-game that supervisors permit supervisees to pursue, then they are completely missing the point and failing in their duty.

In supervision as in each of the caring professions 'there are no perfectly safe helping relationships, as there are always risks of transgressions.'[1]

> The 'binary of safe/unsafe and totalising constructions of paralysing risk or perfect safety' need to be challenged by supervisors who 'work to co-create relationships of 'enough-safety' with workers.'[2]

Since supervision is *other* rather than *self*-centred, supervisors play a key role 'in differentiating experiences of being unsafe from being discomforted. Supervisors need to resist prioritising the comfort of practitioners over the actual safety of clients.'[3] Being a guest in supervisees' lives, gives the supervisor the freedom to act on behalf of those outside the room (clients) who could easily be forgotten. Being truly other-centred

> *'our collective commitments to justice-doing require us to unsettle some of the comforting knowledges that help invisibilise our privileges and the subjugation of others those privileges stand on. Discomfort is predictable and possibly necessary.'*[4]

The paradox of supervision – multiplied yet further in group supervision - is that the space has to be 'safe *enough*' to make it possible for supervisees to let their practice be seen while challenging *enough* to allow transformative learning to take place.

> When we make it safe to fail we make it safe to succeed.

Boundaries exist to safeguard against abuse and to enable the good to happen. The perimeter fence around a children's swing park enables safe play within a clearly demarcated space. So too the boundaries we put in place in supervision are there to make soul, role and context conversations possible. And 'while it is the supervisor's responsibility to manage them, supervisees need to be involved in negotiating them.'[5]

To be safe enough to be seen, to learn and to grow, five boundaries need to be negotiated and collectively monitored in group supervision.

1.Boundary of the relationship

Since supervision is intentional rather than casual and regular rather than opportunistic, the relationship between participants needs to be boundaried. This is especially true when dual relationships exist (as in Team, Organizational and Peer supervision) or when participants have social relationships as friends or colleagues outside of supervision. Knowing and respecting the boundary of the supervisory relationship releases the supervisor from being locked into the supervisory role outwith supervision sessions. It also protects supervisees from having to live under the relentless spotlight of their peers outside of the session.

2.*Boundary of content*

Supervision is a work-based conversation which invites reflection on the past in the present for the sake of the future. Having agreed boundaries about the content of supervisory sessions prevents issues more suited to personal therapy, line management or spiritual guidance displacing the reflective task.

3.*Boundary of time*

Establishing time boundaries (and sticking to them) is a profound way of telling people that their lives and other commitments are of value and that the supervisory process can be trusted. Time boundaries include length of sessions, use of time within those sessions and intervals between sessions.

4.*Boundary of space*

Paying careful attention to the physical or online environment by ensuring that the session will not be overheard, interrupted or broadcast to others makes meaningful conversation possible. A lackadaisical attitude to the environment (for example meeting in a cluttered room or live streaming your family preparing dinner in your kitchen while you are engaging in supervision) does nothing to suggest the quality of space that supervision promises.

5.*Boundary of confidentiality*

Negotiating the parameters of confidentiality (including its limits) is all part of fostering an atmosphere conducive to learning. Will notes be taken and if so for what purpose? Will feedback be offered to anyone who is not in the room? Who else will come to hear about what was aired, shared or discovered etc..[6]

Keeping it simple

Boundaries are what makes freedom possible. We build them around things we value and around things we wish to protect. The co-creation and monitoring of boundaries in group makes the good possible and mitigates against costly carelessness.

Cultivating courage

Porous boundaries
will not serve the task of reflection.
If I am to take risks
I need to know that I will be met
I need to know that my courage
will be greeted with empathy
I need parameters within which
I can discern an appropriate level of sharing
Your invitation to take a leap
must be fenced around
to contain my response
And the brave space we create together
must be a temporary installation
readily dismantled when our work is done
and easily resurrected
for our next round of reflexive engagement.
Boundaries enable risk.

Note 30 Contracting

'Politeness is the poison of collaboration'
Edwin Land

Establishing clarity of expectation among group members, while crucial, is only one aspect of contracting since others also have a stake in what happens. A group of colleagues, for example, may see themselves as sufficiently self-aware to not require a named supervisor whereas their employers or the statutory bodies behind them may insist that a qualified and accredited supervisor does so. Similarly a supervision group may wish to be cross-professional in make up only to find that when push comes to shove, some of the professions from which group members come will only allow them to record uni-professional supervision sessions.

Contracting requires negotiation between the potentially competing expectations of

> Supervisors.
> Supervisees.
> The agency or organization.
> Wider stakeholders.

As a supervisor I might want to offer everyone creative forms of supervision whereas the agency that hires me to supervise their staff might want me to engage in case presentations and reviews.

Group participants might want to explore what they bring in smaller groups of two or three people whereas I, as supervisor, might prefer to work with the group as a whole.

And the agency might warm to non-disclosive supervisory methods (such as those described in the story about the jug that needed topping up in Note 22) whereas the professional body responsible for the registration and revalidation of their staff might need evidence of themes explored and safeguarding monitoring.

I alluded earlier to issues around how long group sessions should be, how frequently groups should meet and how participation can be logged (Note 17). The various stakeholders involved may each have their own views on such questions which cannot be ignored.

As a rule of thumb, it is good practice to ask before agreeing to supervise a group whether what you offer (and this may include your qualifications) will be acceptable or in fact disenfranchise potential supervisees. The supervision you offer may be outstanding but if participants (who need to) cannot log it then you have a problem.

Be careful finally not to get caught in closed loop systems. Taking anyone into a group with no feedback loop to the organization may appeal to supervisees but it may cause you some headaches especially when you have first-hand evidence of incompetence or dangerous practice which puts those with whom supervisees work at risk. When working for a team or organization putting in place a simple service level agreement may offer sufficient protection. Such agreements may simply report that you met, you explored a work-based issue that was alive for the person and that you have no safeguarding concerns. Better to have such a loop-back system in place that you never need to use than none at all when you do.

The following sample contract is an amalgamation of various sources and is offered to stimulate your own thinking. It should be critically adapted for your own specific contexts.

Sample Supervision Contract

Supervisor & Supervisees contact details
Number of sessions agreed Duration of sessions
Fee arrangements
Missed Appointments

Understanding of Supervision

Supervision supports practitioners to give the best of themselves to those with whom they work. It does this through monitoring their competence and fitness to practice, expanding their skill base and professional growth and by offering a safe space to discharge feelings, explore difficulties and re-energise their practice. Supervision plays an ongoing role in turning practice into learning and experience into wisdom. The goal of supervision is improved well-being of both the practitioner and those in their care.

Ethical Stance

My practice as a supervisor is governed by the Code of Conduct of ....
If you have concerns about my practice you should contact ...

As supervisor and supervisees, we agree

- That we will take care to respect the importance of confidentiality, within certain specified and agreed limits.
- That the aims of our sessions are to enable us to reflect on issues affecting practice, in order to develop personally and professionally, and to improve and sustain high quality of practice.
- That we will meet once every ... weeks for two hours, in privacy and with no interruptions.
- That we will give the sessions high priority in our diaries, and only reschedule in exceptional circumstances.

- That we will agree what documentation, if any, will be kept of our meetings, and who will have access to this.
- That we will agree the duration of this contract, and/or when it should be revised or reviewed.

As supervisee I agree to

- Come prepared for the session, and bring work-based material for reflection.
- Take responsibility for making effective use of time.
- Take responsibility for the outcomes and actions I take as a result of supervision.

As supervisor I agree to

- Offer you attentive listening, support, and constructive challenge, to enable you to reflect on practice, and to develop the skills necessary for practising more effectively.
- Take responsibility for co-ordinating the sessions by booking agreed venue, and managing the boundaries.
- Keep all information you reveal in supervision confidential, unless you reveal any unsafe, unethical or illegal practice. In the event of such disclosures, I will counsel you to deal with the issue yourself through appropriate channels, check that this has been done, and if not, and only having informed you that I intend to do so, as a last resort, reveal the information to the appropriate authorities.
- Use my own supervision for ongoing development of the skills and knowledge necessary for becoming more effective in my practice, and so be better able to support you in my role as supervisor.

Additional clauses specific to our context

Signed (supervisee) date Signed (supervisor) date

Keeping it simple

Agreements keep the space clean and clear and make good work possible. Disagreements get in the way leaving debris in their wake. Let's agree to agree and let's agree what to do when we don't.

Making the implicit explicit

It's easy to be seduced by the notion
that, in a room full of adults
it is safe to rely on
good intentions
and shared values
and common purpose
Yet the unspoken contracts
are often the ones
that cause us most grief
tripping us up
when we least expect
and when we're most invested
Articulating roles and rules
Negotiating desires and expectations
taking nothing as read
lays the foundation
of hospitality
the bedrock on which
supervision is practiced and sustained.
Clarity is an act of hospitable love.

Note 31 Dynamics in Group Supervision

'Supervision is a container for creativity and chaos.'
Steve Page & Val Wosket[1]

Dynamics have been identified and continuously addressed throughout this book: dynamics in our families of origin which echo in groups throughout our lives; dynamics which enable and dynamics which impede the supervisory relationship; dynamics which arise from the experience and professional development of participants; dynamics which arise from the various styles of group supervision on offer, from the various stakeholders and from the chosen modalities.

Dynamics are a given in every group and context and as such are informants. They shine the spotlight on matters which require attention. They reveal underlying issues. They offer wisdom which is waiting to be unwrapped. As such supervisors can expect dynamics to pop up continuously in supervision and therefore need to develop their antennae for recognizing what they call us to attend to and how best to do so.

The four main categories of dynamics in group supervision are:

> dynamics arising from the conduct of the supervisor
> dynamics arising from the supervisory context
> dynamics arising from the group's interactions with each other
> dynamics arising within the supervisory material.

Dynamics arising from the conduct of the Supervisor

When a group senses a gap in leadership, for example when a supervisor places their need to belong and to merge with the group and abdicates their role authority in holding the group, group members, sensing the leadership vacuum can arise as alternative leaders. Those whose bids are successful are likely to bring their allies with them leaving other contenders envious or simply disengaged. Supervisors also contribute negatively to the group dynamic when they are inconsistent in their engagement of the group by showing partiality to some members and neglect to others or by having A star participants whose insights are publicly validated and remedial supervisees whose contributions are sidelined.

Lew and Bettner (1995) identify four Crucial C's that supervisors need to be aware of in group situations. Each person in the group needs to feel that:

> They belong and therefore can *Connect.*
> They have resources and are therefore *Capable.*
> They are significant and therefore they *Count.*
> They can face difficulties with *Courage.*[2]

According to Lew and Bettner (1995), these needs are 'so crucial that if not met in constructive ways [participants] will find other less useful ways of achieving them in groups.'

A supervisor will have gone a long way to ensure that their presence and style contribute positively to the group's life and purpose if they are mindful that they are there to foster the 4 C's

- to help individuals *connect* with their life giving purpose (soul); to connect with each other and to connect with the supervisory purpose (reflection which results in a response back in the world of practice);
- to bring out the *capable*, 'can do', wisdom of the group
- to conduct the session in such a way that hospitality and opportunity are offered equally and not partially since every member *counts*
- and to foster above all by modelling *courage* which enables group mem-

bers to face the future with hope.

In my experience, some of my failures with groups, especially with groups of insightful, committed practitioners who bring an element of playful imagination to supervision, is that I wanted to be their peer and was ambivalent about being their supervisor. I wanted to be included in the gang and not have to play the adult. Recalling such experiences I find this reminder very salutary: the relationship between supervisor and supervisees is not symmetrical. It is characterised by mutuality, reciprocity and equality but not by symmetry.[3]

Dynamics arising from the Supervisory Context

When supervision is mandated rather than voluntarily entered into, supervisors and supervisees can find themselves embroiled in a 'stuck' dynamic in which those who are keen to get started and invest can feel thwarted by the lack of engagement of their less keen peers. Effective supervisors do well to bring participants' feelings about being mandated to engage in supervision out into the open in the very first session and to explore how the group intends to manage this less than promising situation.

In similar vein, groups who have no say in who will supervise them may well bring a whole tranche of transferential dynamics to the group some of which may enable connection and reflection while others may make the task challenging if not impossible. Groups comprising a range of practitioner experience and/or diverse levels of self-awareness and reflexivity may also create dynamics of their own.

Group style can cause tensions: in team and peer groups, who gets to play the supervisor? In collaborative groups how do you balance the various roles? And in authoritative groups, how do you foster practitioner autonomy without stunting practitioner growth?

A further dynamic arises when reporting or feedback is built into supervision. Supervisors can only report what they see – true – but that leaves supervisees having to negotiate how much of themselves they can bear to be seen. The need to bring whatever material is uppermost for a practitioner at any given time rather than only that which presents them in a good light to the supervisor and/or the rest of the group is something supervisors need to monitor.

In the context of Team, Peer or Organizational supervision, a particular dynamic arises when a supervisee wishes to explore something in which those in the room are implicated. This presents challenging dynamics since a straight narration of the story may be out of the question and even a sanitised (no names and identifying characteristics) presentation may leave others recognising the characters, roles and features being explored. When that happens peers can become unavailable as they dig into entrenched positions which close down the possibility of reflection. Not all is lost, however, especially if supervisors are able to facilitate non-disclosive 'story-telling' forms of supervision such as the Four Elements or working with small world installations or the Inner Wise Guide approach.[4]

Dynamics arising from Group Interaction

For all the reasons we explored when looking at family echoes in groups (see Notes 6 and 7), participants do not usually approach groups from a stance of neutrality. Some come seeking repair, some fearing repeat: all come not knowing how things will unfold. As groups begin, people form ideas about who is in and who is out (centrality and liminality), who is near and who is far (influence and power) and who is up and who is down (hierarchy and inferiority).

Groups which skirt around these dynamics at the beginning and launch straight into exploring work-based issues that members bring, fool themselves if they think that dynamics are not present because we are all adults, or because we are too mature for that childish stuff to play out here. Bidden or unbidden, dynamics are present and supervisors who underplay their importance let both themselves and the group down.

> *'Supervision groups stimulate transferences and projections, both toward the supervisor and between the group members. Exposing one's*

> *difficulties and shortcomings, not only to the supervisor but also to the others in the group, may be accompanied by feelings of shame, just as success may result in collegial competition and rivalry.'*[6]

In individual supervision we encounter bidirectional transferences which arise between two parties. In group supervision we face multidirectional transferences which could be coming not only from each of the participants and the supervisor but from each of the groups, organizations and systems behind them.[7] Transferences and projections in groups may well have their origins in needs not met in our families of origin. Forms of acting out which interrupt the group or prevent it from actually achieving its reflective task may stem from childhood needs for recognition and from a person's need to be recognized. If they cannot be recognised for their positive contribution then they may resort to developing a reputation for being notorious. Eg. 'If I can't be reflective like these other people or insightful or have wise contributions to offer and feedback to give or even interesting cases or material to present I can be recognized as 'the thwarter', the nuisance, the one who makes everyone laugh or simply the one everyone rejects.'

Even in highly functioning groups characterised by high levels of self-awareness and investment in the supervisory process, dynamics will arise between group members which need to be treated for what they are: sources of information that something of importance is calling for the group's attention.

> dynamics are sources of information that something of importance is calling for the group's attention

A loss of energy in the group, a change in the way the group 'normally' interacts with each other, a contribution offered with best intentions that is received as persecutory or insulting are not signs of dysfunction in a group but rather of authentic engagement. If participants have been helped at the beginning of a session to make room within them for the group and for the reflective process then anything that starts to look or feel like a departure from boundaried, open, hospitality can be trusted as the unconscious trying to break through.[8] Sometimes that dynamic points to something 'homeless' or as yet waiting to be owned by the supervisee. As Greenhalgh (2000) writes: 'provocations and projections enable others in the group to feel things which they have not felt before, and rediscover aspects of themselves which have been projected or denied'.[9]

Dynamics arising from the Supervisory Material

Here is an illustration of dynamics which can arise out of the material being explored in group supervision.

> Tracy was telling the group about her two new colleagues that had recently been recruited. After working solo for three months she said that it was a relief to have colleagues again and that the future looked bright. When she had finished, the supervisor asked group members to say what they had noticed as they had listened to Tracy. 'I noticed that on the face of it you told us a good news story but I was struck that you told it in a very flat voice.' 'I noticed that you had really wanted to have these colleagues but sensed a gap between the rhetoric and the reality now that you actually have them'. Others spoke in similar terms.
>
> Returning to the supervisee, the supervisor asked: 'Does anything you have heard resonate with you Tracy?' Tracy turned red with anger. 'Why are you all raining on my parade? This is what always happens to me. Just when I get something good someone undermines it.'
>
> The group fell silent. After a while the supervisor asked: 'What if the group is not raining on your parade Tracey. What if the group is actually investing in your parade by what they are offering you?'
>
> Tracey paused, took a deep breath and sat with her thoughts for a while. Breaking her silence she said: 'I've just realised that I moaned so much about being on my own for so long that I now feel

> obliged to say it's great to have colleagues – but the truth that I haven't really been able to admit, even to myself, is that I am having to find my own voice again and work out who I am in the new shiny team. I think the group is on to something I was trying to keep the lid on.'

A number of factors are key to that example.

1. The supervisor was working collaboratively with the group.
2. At no point did the supervisor offer an authoritative interpretation of what was going on for the supervisee but simply invited the group to name the impact of the story upon them.
3. When the supervisee became emotive and lashed out at the group, the supervisor did not retaliate or become defensive.
4. On the basis of the impact the story had on group members the supervisor had the courage to invite the supervisee to revisit rather than discount the feedback she had instinctively rejected.
5. Withstanding the temptation to brush awkward feelings and emotions under the carpet led to significant insights for the supervisee about what was really going on.

Keeping it simple

Dynamics are a given in every group. They shine a light on issues which require attention. They reveal underlying issues. The job is not to eradicate them but to detect their presence and tease out their meaning.

Waving a baton

Conducting an orchestra
involves bringing in the right parts
at the right time
attending to dynamics
giving clear signals
Not too distant from group facilitation
Careful attention to detail
Clarity of purpose
being careful to articulate
even the, perhaps reasonable, assumption
that all those present
with perhaps a reasonable assumption
that all those present
share the same intention:
to make beautiful music.
An unspoken
yet powerful contract
to which all participants must adhere.
Until the percussionist
decides to claim more airtime
Or the tuba player attempts to drown out the trumpets
while the violas refuse to follow the rhythm set by the cellos
The hapless conductor becomes pulled this way and that
with only the flutes and clarinets
making any effort to comply with the orchestration
until everyone leaves in a cacophony of confusion.

Note 32 Characters in Groups

'Don't get confused between my personality and my attitude.
My personality is who I am, my attitude depends on who you are.'
Frank Ocean

One of my supervisees, a pastor, developed the art of speaking about the characters in her congregation in very discreet terms. 'My congregation is made up of three categories of people: some I would say are original; some are unique and some are truly remarkable.' 'Yes, Peggy your husband is certainly original. And to have been married to him these last forty years makes you utterly remarkable.' The use of such coded language meant that none of her congregation could ever work out whether she was paying a complement or indicating how off the wall she thought they actually were!

Life is full of characters. Groups too! One of my practices after meeting with an in-person group for the first time is to walk around the room, recalling each face and name, and getting a sense of that person's personality, their presence and their way of being in the group. Working online I do something similar remembering each face in its digital box.

Many of the characters who pitch up in groups are indeed unique. Others are variations on caricatures.

- There is the Teacher's Pet, the self-appointed co-supervisor who assumes the role at the drop of a mitre.
- There's the Commandant who hides behind seniority or length of service

dispensing wisdom and instruction.

- There's the Group Lawyer who cites policy and procedure and keeps the group in fear.
- The Citizen's Advice agent who compulsively wants to fix everybody.
- The Kleenex agent who wants to wipe away anything emotional.
- The Bomber who throws a grenade just when there is no room to safely detonate it.
- Mr and Mrs Absent who draw attention to themselves even when present.
- Dead man/woman walking
- Job's comforters
- and a whole host of other characters besides who show up in all kinds of groups, supervision included.

Much of the time such characters can be managed within the group dynamic and process but some, with varying levels of intentionality, obfuscate the group's reflexive process. The Smiling Saboteur presents as charming and 'only wanting to be helpful' but ensures that nothing of value will be found in the session and tricks others into ensuring that such prophecy is fulfilled. The Caustic Cynic gave up on hope a long time ago and is certainly not going to be disproved in this group of helpless hopefuls. And there's Fake Jake who couldn't give a toss about anyone else but has learned to pass as genuine, 24/7.

Supervisors beware. It is not your role to convince the unconvinced that supervision works or that reflection is worthwhile. And it is certainly not your role to provide a stage and a platform on which your various characters can act out and rehearse their over familiar dramas. Your role is to host reflexive conversations for original, unique and truly remarkable participants. And if the charade begins, smile. Smile but don't abdicate responsibility for the role for which you have been cast. If you do, you can be sure that there is an understudy waiting in the wings only too ready to change the script and redirect the entire performance.

John Towler (2001) reminds us, that we who supervise are also characters in the group plot. 'Which sub-personality is supervising today?' he asks.[1]

- The Crusader supervisory personality kicks in when supervisors feel the need to protect supervisees from their managers, employers or uncaring organizations. Mistaking empathy for collusion, crusading supervisors metaphorically play the role of shop steward and join the picket lines protesting for better deals.
- Rambo kicks in when the only way to tackle something difficult is to work ourselves into a sweat, armour ourselves up and annihilate the cause of our distress with violent thoughts, words or actions.
- Sherlock Holmes shows up in sessions when supervisors play the detective card, searching for clues, pursuing details and trying to solve mysteries.

The supervisory task is not to be a wallflower, or to conceal all aspects of your own personalty but rather to notice what gets triggered by the various characters in your groups and then to take the finger off the weapon and meet them with hospitality and compassion.

Keeping it simple

Supervision groups are microcosms of life in all its variety. Supervisees and supervisors alike may be truly original, unique and remarkable. Staying curious about ourselves and others is a supervisory asset.

Stay curious

Stay curious
about the group member whose aura of resentment
hangs around them like a halo
Stay curious
about the one who claims all the air space
Stay curious
about the one whose desire is to please
Stay curious
about the one who sucks life out of others' joy
Stay curious
to these and more
For each has a story.
Staying curious enables that story to be told
With curiosity comes insight
With insight comes acceptance
With acceptance comes potential for change
Stay curious!

Note 33 Help! I'm Stuck!

'Before Alice got to Wonderland she had to fall pretty hard down a deep hole.'
Lewis Caroll

How many times have I heard supervisees tell me that they are stuck? How many times have I wanted to say 'me too'? What I learned from embodied approaches to supervision is the value of inviting supervisees who claim to be stuck to indicate just how stuck they are: completely stuck (as in frozen or paralysed)? or just a little bit stuck (as in 'I can't wiggle my fingers but my legs still work)? Asking supervisees to show how stuck they are in embodied ways (by taking a stance in the body or by expressing it in heir hands or face when working online) gives the supervisor an indication of the perceived gravity of the situation. Similarly asking supervisees to say what would happen if they were *not* stuck can reveal the intention, the thing that they are looking for in exploring the situation.

Finding ourselves stuck as supervisors is often an indication that we have forgotten that our role is not to fix but to accompany, not to resolve but to reflect. Nevertheless when being stuck happens in group supervision a number of possibilities are at the supervisor's disposal.

If the presenting supervisee is willing to embody the stuckness by adopting a posture, the group can then be invited to copy that posture which the supervisee can then observe. Seeing their 'stuckness' embodied by the group, the presenting supervisee can modify it in a manner akin to giving stage directions: 'not that stuck ... more stuck than that'. Participants can then be invited to speak out of the embodied stance 'I hate being in this position'; 'My feet feel glued to the floor'; 'I just want to walk away and sit down'.

Stuckness can arise from a number of places including

- from unresolved material in the supervisee's early patterning. 'That's what I do. I make things better. I've done it all my life so why is it not working now?'
- from contextual factors in which individuals or systems have a vested interest in things not changing 'Management won't allow that so there's no point in me trying it.'
- from a deep recognition that the soul cannot find expression in this role or context 'I used to find such fulfilment in my work but all I do now is go through the motions'.
- from actually having choices that would release me from being stuck but for which I lack the courage to respond (I know I would be free if ... but I can't because...).

> Stuckness can also be a signal from the system that things are not well. Systems that operate on a 'tried that, done that, got the T shirt and it didn't work' basis are actively invested in damming the energetic flow. John Whittington suggests asking the question: 'For who in this system' [team, organization] 'are these words true – "this feels stuck".'

Working in a group provides the opportunity for a supervisee to identify the characters involved. For example 'choose a spot in the room which represents the stuckness' (supervisee could choose a piece of furniture, a cloth or a person to indicate that) 'now place yourself in relation to the stuckness.' (The Supervisee might be invited to experiment with physical proximity and distance and possibly, to speak from each place 'you are too near, I am moving away' 'you've dominated the picture for long enough I refuse to look at you'.) What you are doing through such creative modalities is enabling an internalised or systemic drama to be externalised such that it can be seen through the observing eye. Continuing in this mode you could ask the supervisee to choose something to represent what release (unstuck) would look like. And then to ask 'If this is the answer, what's the question?'[1]

Every system, every organization and every work team has secrets which 'create inertia, resistance to change' and stuckness. Not naming them is exactly how a person stays loyal to them in ways which often parallel the lengths they were to prepared to go as children to belong to their families.

> Every system creates and embodies its own truth. There is a secret sentence embedded in every system.

Individual secret sentences may include: 'Secretly I treat this organization as if it were my family'; 'Secretly I wish they would make me redundant'; Secretly I would make a better supervisor than you'.

Team versions include: 'we call ourselves a team, but secretly, we don't believe it'; Secretly, we have a team leader but we all compete for the position'; 'It's called group supervision but secretly we ridicule it outside of the sessions'.

Supervisor's secret sentences might take the form of 'How lovely to see you all again, but secretly I don't know why I bother'; 'Today is a chance to find insight, but secretly there's little chance of that with you lot'; 'Secretly I don't think much of your skills or self-awareness'.[2]

The problem with such secrets is that they inherently contain reasons why things are likely to stay stuck, why no change can be envisioned and why hope is thwarted. Supervision has the word change written all the way through it. We meet to connect and to reflect with the intention of responding to what we find outside of the session. Supervision as a practice is an agent of change. Stuckness and change are not comfortable bed-fellows. Supervisors who are willing to work dynamically in groups have options. Becoming stuck yourself may at first glance seem like empathy with the presenting supervisee but may in fact be a sign that you have closed the necessary gap between caring and merging. Recover enough distance to see things from the observer stance and then do whatever it takes to respectfully assure stuckness that is has been seen, felt and honoured but it's now time to make room for underdeveloped roles to be brought in and for the stuckness to be released.

Keeping it simple

Feeling stuck brings us up against our own limitations. Supervisors need to mind the gap between caring and merging with their supervisees. Two stuck people leaves no one to lower the ladder into the ditch or call for additional help.

Change at the core

Like a stick of seaside rock
However supervision is presented on the outside
Change is at its centre
We may change the colour
or alter the flavouring
But we cannot escape that consistent core
that trades reporting for reflection
enabling movement
facilitating change
We may gnaw away at the edges
with our words and our thoughts
But, sometimes, plunging in creatively
is the only way to move from stuckness
and experience transformation
that leads to change.
Don't settle for anything less
than supervision that has change at its centre.

Note 34 Reviewing the Life of a Group

'Only ever look back to see how far you have come.'

Reviewing the life of a group is an act of care and respect. Too often energy is spent at the initial contracting stage of a group's life but once that is done and dusted it all gets forgotten. The literature of individual supervision offers a variety of tools for reviewing. The literature of group supervision less so. Of those which do, few include any reference to the life cycle of the group itself.

Using Notes 6 and 7 of this book, group supervisors could review the life of the group after five or six meetings in terms of how unresolved and integrated aspects of participants' early lives have played out. Is the group fundamentally engaged in repeat patterns of interaction characterised by a tendency to react rather than reflect, to retaliate rather than embrace difference? Or is it engaged in reparative patterns of interaction which lead the group to reflect, rehearse and re-envision?[1]

Similarly the group review could be based on how the group has handled its own hatches, matches, scratches and dispatches in the light of which it could attend to unfinished business that impedes its ongoing development (Note 9).[2]

The group could review its life in relation to Lew and Bettner's four C's asking how they belong and can *Connect*; have resources and are *Capable*; are significant and *Count*; and can face difficulties with *Courage*.[3] With as much truth-telling as participants can manage, gaps between rhetoric and reality can be named and group accomplishments celebrated.

Any of the soulful approaches to group supervision outlined in Part Four of this book could be used to review the group's ethos. How do giving and receiving play out in the group? How is reciprocity and mutuality expressed. Do the *givers* also receive? Do the *takers* also give? (Note 37)[4] What about the aspirations expressed in the 'Nine Beats of the Beatitudes'? Can the group 'acknowledge what is broken?' How are they 'using power for good'? Are they able to 'look with compassion'? (Note 38)

Supervisors might also like to review their own contribution to a group's life and perhaps share that with participants. Louie Gardiner's seven attitudes for group ethos offers a wonderfully succinct review tool: 'Am I attuned to Self?; Do I serve the intention? Do I Hold the space and work the edges? Do I dare to call things out?' (Note 39).[5]

Finally, Nancy Kline's 'Ten Components of a Thinking Environment' offer a framework for group exploration. She writes:

> 'The quality of everything we do depends on the quality of the thinking we do first. The quality of our thinking depends on the way we treat each other while we are thinking. The ten behaviours or conditions that generate the best kind of thinking are: Attention, Equality, Ease, Appreciation, Encouragement, Information, Feelings, Diversity, Incisive Questions, Place.'[6]

Applied to supervision, a group could review the 'quality of thinking', of interaction and exploration which characterises the group's experience.

- What quality of *attention* do group members pay each other?
- To what extent are participants truly *equal* in the group? Are some characters more dominant than others?
- To what extent do participants feel at *ease*, able to relax into the space and experience the playfulness it offers?
- Are all contributions *appreciated* or are some valued over others?
- To what extent does the group offer a restorative and encouraging experience? Is the balance between *encouragement* and challenge healthy?

- How does the group share information?
- And what about *feelings*? Are they welcome, discouraged or mandatory within the group ethos?
- How does the group handle *diversity*, especially the more subtle forms of differences? Are differences tolerated, celebrated, played down or amplified?
- Is group life characterised by *incisive* or banal questions? Are the assumptions underlying engagement collusive and avoidant or marked by professional courage and appropriate risk taking?
- Finally how does the group attend to *place* and the physical (or online) environment in which it meets? Is the environment itself conducive to learning, to hospitality and authentic presence?

A group could read Nancy Kline's ten components and self select those characteristics which they can affirm and celebrate, those which are noticeable by their absence and those which are work in progress. As with all review mechanisms, the quality of the interaction between group members is every bit as important as the results found.

Keeping it simple

We review and revisit things that have value: memories, holidays, relationships. We review and revisit on significant anniversaries. We also review when anticipating loss or experiencing grief. Reviewing group life and relationships is a way of saying that groups matter, we matter, it matters.

Staying on track

We made a covenant
Each contributing to its evolving
It was a pulsing energy to which we all ascribed
It worked well as we began
And we referred to it from time to time
Then, as we became familiar with one another
we let things slide
We engaged in collusion because we liked each other
and wanted to preserve our social alliance
Our enjoyment of meeting in group
was not diminished
Indeed it continued to grow
But we lost our focus
Our clarity of purpose
And the work in which we engaged
to which we remained committed
became performative, sometimes restorative
and no longer transformative
Making each other feel good
became more important than reflecting on practice
and we were, after all, juggling some tough gigs
We settled in
and settled down
and settled for less
losing out
through our failure to review.

Note 35 Endings in Groups

'Every time you say goodbye I die a little'
Cole Porter

The way groups end is often foreshadowed by how they begin. Think back to those who struggled to say hello in the early sessions? Have they managed to 'join' the group or has the inevitability that it will end made investing in the group not worthwhile? Who struggled to say goodbye at the end of the first session? Who were the door handle clingers, always last to leave? Who were the Zoom ghosts who were still there when everyone else had gone? And how are they faring as the group approaches its ending.

And what about the surprises? Which participants have made huge personal and professional journeys during the group's life span? And what about those who broke the binary repeat/repair patterns and have experienced new life in the group? How will they be as closure approaches? How are they faring as the group approaches its ending?

> *'If the group has done good work together it will have become a significant life experience for the supervisees. Disruptions and endings can cause grief and anxiety which seem out of proportion for a 'task group'. The supervisor, who may already be gearing up for the next 'intake', should take time to appreciate the ending (or change) of this human system. Coming changes or group demise should be signalled well ahead and suitable leave-taking rituals co-operatively planned.'*[1]

> Good endings are those in which a person has the chance to say four things: Thank you. I'm sorry. I release you from the past. I wish you well for the future.

Some endings are like Velcro, in which one party sticks to the other and will not let go. Some are so loose or casual that there is little evidence that an ending has actually taken place. Some endings have all the hallmarks of grief with one or other party feeling a void opening up within them.

Cut and run endings are those in which supervisees cannot make the final meeting or the one before that and simply disappear without trace.

Their close cousin 'bin bag' endings are those in which the relationship seems to be dumped in a black plastic bag like garbage as if the relationship had no value whatsoever.

Good endings in supervision are those which have been mutually negotiated rather than sprung on one party by the other. With sufficient planning, time can then be set aside to name what has been shared and experienced, the good and the bad.

Good endings are also proportionate to the relationship, the context, and the persons involved. Ending a four-week supervisory relationship with a group of students on placement may feel very different from ending a relationship with a group you have accompanied for several years.

The invitation to say 'thank you' needs to be taken up on both sides. Supervisors who are at home in their own skin are able to name what supervisees have taught them and how the work has nudged them along in their own process as persons and practitioners.[2]

Supervisors should be mindful that their handling of endings within the supervisory relationship will model – for good or for bad – how supervisees might handle endings in their working relationships. All the more reason then, to ensure that goodbye means goodbye and that the ending is not fudged or avoided or ambiguous.[3]

Keeping it simple

Ending well starts by beginning well. From then on every session offers hints of how the ending might be. Watch. Note. Stay curious. Good hosts know as much about saying goodbye as they do about saying hello.

With the end in sight

Wisdom proclaims
that in every ending
is a new beginning
The space between
calls for a ritual of acknowledgement
and reassurance
to ensure that the tasks of moving on
are oiled with the same care
as the work already accomplished
Remembering that the ending
is pre-figured in the beginning
and honed in every session
prepares the way
for groups to be willing
to embark on new discoveries
with different companions
for a new season of reflection
In every ending
a new beginning.

V

Part Five Soulful Supervision

Note 36 Resonance over Relevance

'We spend so much of our lives waiting for our souls to catch up.'
Carol Perry [1]

The literature of supervision is liberally seasoned with the word *space*. Sometimes supervision is referred to as 'safe space', sometimes as 'brave space'. Naming supervision as such to trainee supervisors results in heads nodding in agreement. Everyone agrees in theory but in practice keeping the space *spacious* can be very hard work indeed.

Beginning supervisors often fill the supervision space with anxiety. Before the group even arrives they might be asking themselves: 'What if no-one comes?'; 'What if they all come and they all want to present something? How will we fit everyone in to the allotted time?' And then once the session is underway yet more space can be taken up by the supervisor wondering 'What if I have nothing to say or offer in response to this presentation?' Keeping the space spacious and uncluttered can be hard work indeed.

I wonder if at root our struggles as supervisors to create space in supervision comes down to issues of relevance and resonance. I was trained to pursue relevance - to try to piece things together and see how they connect - but have come to see the transformation that comes from pursuing resonance and what causes reverberations in the soul.

Focus on Relevance

A relevant approach to supervision acts out of the belief that the more the supervisor and the group understands the situation being presented the more helpful they will be to the supervisee. The focus on relevance is set from the very outset of the session by supervisors who conduct supervision along these lines:

- 'Who in the group has something they would like to reflect on today?'
- 'Thanks Zac. Off you go, tell us the story.'
- 'Can I just check that I've got this right.'
- 'So the characters are ... and they did ... and then you said ... and then what happened was ...'

What happens in this pursuit of 'relevance' is that an underlying assumption is allowed to go unchecked. That underlying assumption is that the more the supervisor and supervisees *understand* the story (by piecing details together), the more helpful they will be. Not so, says Nancy Kline since what may seem relevant (and even interesting) to everyone else in the room is likely to be already deeply familiar (and possibly even boring) to the supervisee.[2] What is more, precious time is being taken up in information exchange to the detriment of finding fresh insight.

Focus on Resonance

A resonant approach to supervision stems from a belief that the stories supervisees bring to supervision are *not* in fact the material they want to explore but simply the bearers of that material. As such, a resonant approach to supervision arises from the deep conviction that what people typically bring to supervision are aspects of their lives in which the soul is having to negotiate how to express itself in a given role and context. The subtlety of such an approach is that relevance is relocated from what the *group* considers to be relevant (background, context, missing information etc.) to what *reverberates* in the supervisee's soul and is therefore ultimately relevant for them.

The focus on resonance is once again set from the very outset of the session by supervisors who conduct supervision along these lines:

- 'Who in the group has something they would like to reflect on today?'
- 'Thanks Zac. Before you tell us what you are bringing, do you know why this issue matters to you?'
- 'Ok, what do we need to know in order to support your reflections today?'
- 'How does this sit with your values ... or sense of yourself ... or your soul?'
- 'What's the most important thing you have heard yourself say ... or felt since we started?'
- 'What is this reflection touching for you? What are you finding?'

Supervision which focuses on resonance recognizes that the world of work often leaves supervisees so busy that they need time for their souls to catch up.[3] Life is lived, experiences are had but meaning is missed. Work gets done but connection with the underlying purpose that makes the work worthwhile wears thin.

Listening for resonance is akin to listening to the long reverberations which emanate from singing bowls. Try it for yourself and you will see how the sound waves continue for quite some time. The effect of slowing things down and not speaking until each sound has come to an end beautifully illustrates the pursuit of resonance in supervision.

Keeping it simple

Sound a singing bowl or play one online. Pause and listen to how long it takes for the reverberations to stop. That is the kind of slowed down pace at which resonant supervision operates. And if you are not convinced then try it for yourself in self-supervision.

Resonance

Resonance
Found in the deep bass notes
achieved by laying the fingers
firmly on the strings
and letting the bow dig in
Found, too, in the sweet, high pitch
of a harmonic
called forth by the lightest touch
that gently coaxes out a beauty
that may be lost
to those whose hearing is dulled
by all the background noise
or the tiredness of tuning in
The initial sound
is but a prelude
to the depth that lingers
beneath the surface
or the oscillation
that continues to disturb
long after the sound waves
have stilled
We who listen
are called to go there
Invited to stay
with the ripple that continues
when the movement has stopped.

Note 37 On Giving and Receiving

'I have found that among its other benefits,
giving liberates the soul of the giver.'
Maya Angelou

The radical mutuality and reciprocity of supervision is beautifully expressed by Sheila Ryan who weaves insights from her practice as a homeopath into her practice as a supervisor. She writes:

> *'We meet as people. We take our places: one .. as supervisor, the other .. as supervisee. We make the 'case' together. This is the art-work we create in our relationships; the outcome of story, maps and models, art and craft. .. In 'receiving' another we are accepting what comes. We are open, soft, receptive, feminine. We are forgetting who we are and what we want. In 'taking' from another we are looking for something. We have something in mind. We are focused, hard eyed, hunting, masculine. We are remembering who we are and what we want.'*[1]

I am deeply indebted to Sheila Ryan for highlighting that both postures – giving and receiving – are needed in supervision not in the traditional forms of helper (supervisor) and helped (supervisees) but in that much older wisdom tradition which underlines the truth that our liberation lies in mutuality and reciprocity. In a world which commodifies everything and reduces everyone to the level of consumers, soulful supervision says, let's pause:

> *Let's turn down the volume of the outside world, let's amplify voices that fight to be heard elsewhere and let's call each other to more truth and love.*[2]

So much of our training in the caring professions teaches us to be afraid of each other, to keep our distance. We are actively trained to be afraid. Why else would we take out indemnity insurance against our clients? Of course the public need protected from rogue and unboundaried practitioners, but no code of ethics, no accreditation programme and no amount of supervision will ever do the inner work that makes it possible for supervisors to know who they are, know whose they are and know whose they need to be. That inner work is what makes it possible for those of us who supervise to respond homeopathically which in Sheila Ryan's terms means

> Uniquely – adapting to each new situation.
> Vitally – responding to what's important.
> Similarly – getting alongside the other.
> Minimally – doing just enough to restore freedom.

I am no homeopath but what Sheila Ryan teaches me is that perhaps the role of the supervisor is to be the balancing mineral - the missing element - that is needed in any given situation. On that principle, if the supervisee is hard on themself, the supervisor enlarges their compassion towards them. If the supervisee tends to make everything about themself, the supervisor keeps those in their care in view. Minimal intervention for maximum potency, the hallmark of homeopathy, just about sums up soulful, resonant, reciprocal supervision.

Keeping it simple

If we are truly hospitable as supervisors then we will be met back by our supervisory guests. The reciprocity of supervision, for those open to receive it, results in supervisors not only giving but also receiving from those we host.

Weeding out the competition

Soulful, resonant, reciprocal
Elements that meet rather than compete
That respond rather than react
That enable rather than exchange
Synergising in a shared task
in which all have a part to play
each contribution unique and valued
each a stimulus for the other
working together in the shared intention
of finding meaning for each
that liberates the soul for communion.

Note 38 The Nine Beats

'Hospitality is not about inviting people into our perfect homes.
It's about inviting people into our imperfect hearts.'
Anon

Practitioners tie themselves in knots over issues of neutrality and self-disclosure. 'Agenda free zone' might as well be the notice on the door of the room where some supervisors work. Scratch a little and you will find evidence of lazy thinking which equates creating a space for others (supervisees) with neutrality. But how can supervision be neutral if it is fundamentally relational? How can supervisors be committed if they are agenda free?

Supervision is anything but neutral. On the contrary it has a huge agenda: to support supervisees to be the very best version of themselves so that those *they* support can flourish. In other words supervision supports well-being for everyone involved: well-being for the supervisee; well-being for the 'client' and well-being for the system or organization in which the care or service is provided. It is right that supervisors should resist hijacking sessions with their own agendas but that should not be confused with investing sufficiently in those relationships such that supervisees know that their supervisors want them to thrive.

Within the Christian spiritual tradition, the Beatitudes offer a rhythmic nine-beat pattern for the spiritual journey. As translations of translations they are best known in their passive form: 'Blessed are those who are poor; Blessed are the hungry; Blessed are those who stand up for justice etc..' Research into the original Aramaic, however, suggests that they are far from passive but in fact a call to action: 'Get up, go ahead, do something you who are poor'. 'Get up, go ahead and do something you who are hungry.'[1]

In what follows I offer a riff on the Beatitudes. For the purposes of group supervision this could be used as a form of contracting at the outset of a new supervision group. It could equally be used to set the tone and ethos at the beginning of subsequent supervision sessions or as a tool for reviewing the life of a group four or five sessions on.[2]

> In this supervision space we create together
> may we receive each other with open hearts
> acknowledge what is broken
> serve with dignity
> use power for good
> look with compassion
> walk in honesty
> reach past difference
> practice costly love
> and be courageous.

Keeping it simple

Supervision refuses to accept the status quo. It is directed towards new and better futures based on action. Get up, go ahead, do something! We, the group, will support you!

Attentiveness

Looking for the sights that matter
Listening for truths that are important
Amidst all that wounds and disturbs
Seeing through the glare
Hearing in the cacophony

that quiet thread
that brings focus
in all the distraction
And, in the midst of chaos
discerning the gift
hidden from voyeurs,
the treasure revealed to pilgrims
who leave what they know
to venture beyond the threshold
and are rewarded
with wisdom
not of this world.
Blessed are those eyes
Blessed are those ears.
Blessed are they.

Note 39 Group Ethos

'Don't explain your philosophy. Embody it.'
Epictetus

In *Coaching Supervision Groups* (2022), Louie Gardiner identifies seven behaviours or ways of being to which supervisors and supervisees can aspire.[1] Together they foster an optimum supervisory culture. What she suggests is both generic and applicable in any supervisory context while being specific enough to allow supervisors to own and adapt them according to the groups they supervise. These principles could be used at the group agreement stage (in setting the ethos for the group's work together), at the beginning of a supervision session (to remind participants of their best aspirations for the session), by the supervisor outside of the session (to reflect on how they conducted themselves and/or on the group dynamic) or by the whole group when they come to review or end the work.

> Attune to Self
> Engage with love
> Serve the intention
> Hold the space, work the edges
> Illuminate and explore what is calling for attention
> Dare to call it out
> Attend to the relationships, individual and situational context

Attune to self, reminds supervisors that the most important moment in the session happens before anyone arrives. In making space within ourselves, and deepening our self-awareness of what could impede the hospitality we are about to offer others we, supervisors, open ourselves and yield to the quiet, unhurried, reflexive opportunity which lies before us.

Engage with love is a call to action which begins with compassion towards ourselves and opens out from there to make room for those in the group, bringing goodwill and appreciating the humanity of group members and their desire to do their best.

Serve the intention reminds us that supervision is not random or opportunistic but intentional. We meet to connect, to reflect and to respond. We meet to ensure that those not in the room (our absent others) are best served by what happens in the room.

Hold the space, work with the edges is a shared responsibility. Learning spaces need boundaries and careful holding. Without sufficient safety no one can learn. Without an element of stretching no one grows. Some of the edges will arise from families of origin, some from the group dynamic and some from the material which is presented. Containment allows movement and flow.

Illuminate and explore what is calling for attention keeps the supervisory focus on the *why* which underpins the *what* of the material being presented. Keeping a focus on what the supervisee is hoping to find rather than on the myriad of things which fascinate the supervisor or group members will minimize distraction and maximise the pursuit of insight.

Dare to call it out. Supervision is fuelled by courage. Sometimes the tank is full, sometimes empty. Supervisors can model for group members the courage it takes to face difficult situations or call out less than helpful interpersonal dynamics in the group.

Attend to the relationships, individuals and situational context. Seeing things whole rather than as a series of atomized parts, helps supervisees understand the dynamism between soul, role and context.

Keeping it simple

Ethos is meaningless unless lived out. Be the kind of presence you want the group to mirror back to you. Model it. Review it. Start afresh when you fail.

I want to break free

Breaking free from assigned roles
Relinquishing imposed responsibility
Choosing who I shall be
and how I shall be
in this space
with these people
in this moment
Trying things on for size
Seeing what fits
Like delving into the dressing up box
to emerge with all manner of possibilities
And, while discovering what fits best,
always maintaining flexibility to adapt
to best serve those with whom I work.
Embodying practice
and practicing embodiment.

Note 40 Supervising Barefoot

O child of unnecessary shoes
cast them off and stand in readiness on this holy ground
for the Egypt in people's lives
demands that you see burning bushes all around you
a flame burning wildly
calling you away from the comfort of well protected feet.
Macrina Wiedekehr OSB[1]

In the opening Notes of this book, I challenged traditional approaches to supervision training which begin by looking outwards at how groups behave and interact and which take as their starting point the dynamics between participants. My argument was that although all of this is useful and indeed necessary, it starts in the wrong place. My contention is that

> Supervisors need knowledge (frameworks and theories) they need skills (modalities and interventions) but above all they need personhood and presence.

Making intentional use of themselves in the service of others is an incremental process which grows as frameworks and theories are increasingly absorbed, cease to be self-conscious and are integrated into practice. In similar vein, thinking what to say or do next recedes to the back of awareness as informed and attuned instincts kick in.

The invisible watermark printed across every page of this book says this:

> Supervision is an other-centred activity. Supervisors get out of the way.

Yes supervisors have a role to play but they must not allow themselves to become the centre of attention. Even authoritative groups which are supervisor-led must not become supervisor-centred. As I have repeatedly argued, the centre of attention belongs outside the supervisory room with the absent others that those in the room support.

Some supervisors make themselves the centre of attention and liberally cast their pearls of wisdom before any who will give them a hearing.

Some supervisors find themselves the centre of attention by groups which really value them and which hang on their every word.

And some supervisors find themselves the centre of attention because they hold their role authority and clarity of purpose so well that groups attack them for calling out behaviours or dynamics which bring them up short.

Collusion and avoidance are ubiquitous. Not only are they found in every walk of life but are often also rewarded. For an easier life we habitually turn a blind eye to some of what we see around us. 'Life is too short' we say 'choose your battles', 'choose carefully what's worth going to the stake for'. But isn't it striking how everyday language makes wounding and death the obvious consequence for those who refuse to collude.

Within a supervision session it is highly improbable that anyone is going to die. What is however likely is that a group – or some members of a group – can leave a supervisor fighting for their life. Those who supervise barefoot, who allow themselves to enter the space bravely and who have befriended their own vulnerability rather than clothed it in suits of armour, may well find that some members of their groups simply cannot bear it. Undefended to them equals 'weak'. Vulnerable equals 'unable to hold me'. Fluid and agile equals 'doesn't know what he is doing'. Some of these scripts may be echoes of early family patterning. Some may have been acquired in other supervision groups.

Sometimes the attacks we experience in groups are warranted. 'You said we would all have a chance to bring our work and you have used up all the time on two group members'; 'You said every voice and viewpoint is welcome but you have sidelined mine in favour of hers'. Sometimes 'attack' is the only response a person can access in response to what they perceive between what we promised (our espoused commitments) and our actual practice (operant behaviours): 'you said the sessions were confidential but I know you told my manager what I brought to the last session'; 'you said this was a safe space but what you said a moment ago has left me feeling very small and frightened'.

At such times supervisors have a range of options most of which will not serve the group's reflective purpose. Becoming defensive may well acquit us and prove our 'not guilty' pleas, but it will do nothing for the group member who has challenged us nor will it allow us to model best practice to the rest of the group. Neither will abdicating our role as group facilitators and spending the rest of the session looking after upset participants. Nor will explaining ourselves away by telling the group the stress we are under in our personal lives which may have clouded our judgment and actions.

Under perceived or actual attack, the Barefoot Supervisor[2] has a role to play in modelling how to respond maturely in ways which refuse to do violence either to themselves or to any member of the group. If supervision really is about enlarged or amplified vision then our response to finding ourselves unwillingly the centre of attention in groups has to transcend retaliation, self-justification or power grabs. If we are to remain true to our role as facilitators of learning, then finding ourselves under attack offers an important opportunity to model a way of responding which refuses to allow ourselves to being recruited further into the unfolding drama. Vikki Reynolds writes:

> 'Resisting confrontation, evaluation, judgement and attack in group supervision .. we connect in ethical struggles and offer thoughts on theory and practice that are cautious and tentative that we check

> out with the worker we are hoping to assist.'[3]

Whether justified or not, transferential or real, criticism is likely in supervision. The question is 'How will we manage it?' The French philosopher Michel Foucault lyrically portrays the Barefoot Supervisor's response as follows:

> *I dream about a kind of criticism that would try not to judge but to bring an idea to life; it would light fires, watch the grass grow, listen to the wind, and catch the sea foam in the breeze and scatter it. It would multiply not judgements but signs of existence; it would summon them, drag them from their sleep. Perhaps it would invent them sometimes — all the better. All the better. Criticism that hands down sentences sends me to sleep; I'd like a criticism of scintillating leaps of imagination. It would not be sovereign or dressed in red. It would bear the lightning of possible storms.*[4]

Keeping it simple

Supervising barefoot with our shoes off renders us vulnerable. It also keeps us grounded. So why stop at shoes? Divesting ourselves of symbols of power - the accreditation certificates which adorn our consulting rooms, the wallets and credit cards in our pockets, the titles we use to describe ourselves - leave us barefoot. What better place from which to authentically relate and reflect together?

Entering the sacred

Hosting a space where vulnerability is encouraged
consists not in being detached
but in being intimately involved
invested in listening
to the spoken and unspoken
noticing dynamics unfolding
remaining curious
open to whatever emerges
For all of it is data
with which to work
And those who recognise the gift
of this sacred work
will find ways to accommodate
all that it demands of a host:
the tentative offerings
to be picked up or discarded
the gentle probing that amplifies metaphor
the focus and alignment
that stays with the energy
and serves to ignite
the gentle spark
that awaits kindling
costly gifts spent
in the service of reflection
hosted on sacred ground.

VI

Part Six Supporting Yourself

Note 41 Self-Care for Supervisors

'Supervisors are injured souls.'
Helena Hargaden[1]

Care for others requires care for self. Just as decorators are likely to go home with paint in their hair and gardeners with soil under their nails, so too, those whose work is in groups which are replete with family echoes, take home invisible imprints on their hearts and minds.[2] That is why self-care is a non-negotiable requirement of ethical practice. It includes supervision on supervision but is more generally expressed in rhythms of work, recreation and rest which are unique to each individual and in which the tyranny of doing 'more' gives way to the sheer luxury of fun, good company and solitude.

> If you truly care about the state of the world, then take time to replenish your spirit. Self-care is not selfish. You cannot serve from an empty vessel.

Self-care could well have been the opening Note in this book since it needs to be well and truly in place long before we know that it is needed and certainly long before we need intensive soul care and time off work. In my experience, self-care for group supervisors takes the following forms:

- Self-care before the group session
- Self-care during the session
- Self-care after the session.

Self-care before the group session

Take time before the group arrives whether in person or online to host and contain yourself. You might like to find something in the room (or take into the room) something that supports your supervisory identity, quietens your jangling mind and harnesses your ability to show up for others. Don't rule out ordinary things which give you a sense of your continuous self: a picture on the wall, a flower, a piece of furniture, a ring on your finger. Ground yourself in whatever way works for you: taking deep breaths, playing gentle music, focusing on something of beauty, light a candle. Give yourself a compassionate team talk; find your size, your voice, your power. Remind yourself what is and what is not yours to do in the session which is about to begin:

> I have come to foster reflection. I have come to harness the group's wisdom. I have not come to take up the air time. I am not here to dispense advice. I am not here to play group referee ...

Notice how you are today: 'I am wobbly like a jelly'; 'I feel rock solid'; 'I am distracted by...' Do whatever it takes for you to be able to say: 'I am brave, I am bruised, this is who I'm meant to be – this is me.'[3] Take time to notice and honour your pre-transferences; your stray thoughts about the group. Notice them without judgment. When you are ready – when you have hosted and contained yourself – and are ready to offer hospitable facilitative presence to others open the door or switch on Zoom and let the participants in.

Self-care during the group session

It is unlikely that you have been the only one who has been engaged in anticipatory feelings about the group session. Since every group carries within it echoes of our families of origin, group participants may be caught in old and unresolved family dynamics just as much as you are. The hallmarks of patterns originating from their families of origin may be unresolved (or homeless) or integrated (housed) and even the most integrated and balanced group members have personality preferences and processing styles which will not always concur with your own

Self-care when a group is midstream calls the overly responsible supervisor back to some home truths:

- everything that happens is information
- the group has a life and a dynamic of its own
- taking everything personally serves no-one and may in fact trigger family of origin dynamics for some group members about inadequate parents or less than sufficient containment.

Be aware that abdicating your role as group facilitator is likely to result in a group member picking up on the leadership vacuum and stepping into the breach. Remaining non-defensive, curious and committed is what will serve the group best. And rather than sending out SOS messages to the group, return to that object, that image, that thing you chose before the session began which grounds and holds you. Touching your wedding ring or adjusting your gaze to take in that card on your desk may be all it takes to know that you are loved and that someone else believes in you. Self-care while a session is in mid-flow is much easier when clarity of identity and responsibility (what is and what is not yours to do) has been established *before* the session began rather than something you find yourself frantically scrambling to assert in the heat of the moment.

Self-care after the group session

Group supervision can be deeply stimulating, professionally energizing and emotionally stretc.hing. When it works well, it can feel like an exhilarating group dive to the depths of the ocean. Such experiences should be savoured. Letting go of what might well constitute the most fulfilling professional experience in any given month will take a lot longer than the time it takes to stack the chairs or to wait for the last Zoom participant to leave the room. At other times, group supervision can be deeply frustrating, professionally testing or emotionally flattening leaving you feeling you need a hot shower to wash it all away. Again self-care is of the essence if you are to neither manipulate the group to brighten up your working day nor demonize them with your catastrophizing feelings between sessions. Options for self-care after the session include

> *Body brush*: Choose a space and brush your body down with your hands, starting with the head and making brisk sweeping movements over the torso and limbs.
>
> *Space clearing*: Strike a singing bowl and listen as it reverberates around the room changing the energies. Or clap your hands as you move around the room claiming your own noise within a room which has been other-focused.
>
> *Changing the Air*: Perhaps the simplest energy changer in town is to open a window at the end of a session and consciously allow what has happened to leave the room as the new air enters.
>
> *Freshening up*: Wash your hands holding your wrists under the cold tap for a while. Notice your own body ground you back in awareness.[4]

Another form of re-centring yourself after group sessions is to make your own 'I was' and 'I am' statements:

- 'I was the supervisor for this group, now I am the man who needs to go shopping for dinner.'
- 'In the group space, I was the recipient of hostile projections, in this space, right now, I remember that I am my partner's beloved.'
- 'In the session, I messed up around x, y, z . Right now in this space, I forgive myself and commit to learning from my mistakes.'

Keeping it simple

Our souls deserve the same level of care that we expend on others. We may attend to that with ritual or with simple affirming practices or statements. However we do it, we owe it to ourselves and to those with whom we work to be as well as we can by practising relentless self-care.

This is me

I step into the room
before anyone else arrives
to make it mine
Or, when the space is already occupied,
I take a moment to breathe my place in it
Claiming the space
Infusing the air with a clarity of purpose
and an aura of intention
Inhabiting this role
with these people
for this time
Then I am ready to share
my gifts and skills
my flaws and vulnerability
as may be demanded
in the task of supervision
And when the last person leaves
I carefully lay down my role
some days shrugging it off gently
other days shaking it off vigorously
And I wander round the room
recalling those who participated
Acknowledging the work we did together
Noting all that I learned
and the things I would rather had been different

I gather up those fragments, storing some for processing later
discarding others that are not mine to carry
And, as I cross the threshold
having done the work of finishing one task
I can then allow my mind to turn
to the next thing on my agenda.

Note 42 Reflecting afterwards

'History is a post-mortem examination.
It tells you how a country died.
But I'd like to know how it lived'
Finley Peter Dunne[1]

Received wisdom suggests that supervisors take notes after working with groups. But before you uncritically swallow that advice, first check your assumptions:

> Why are you inclined to take notes? What is their purpose? Who are they for? What is their focus?

Factual notes/recording what happened

Typically supervisors take notes on what happened, on which supervisee presented in the session, on how the group interacted and on the dynamics which arose. There is certainly a place for that kind of note keeping - as aide memoire - especially at the early stages of development as a group supervisor. But check your assumptions. By the next time you see the group they will have lived a whole lot more of life and are unlikely to be where they were last time you saw them. Check too why you think you need to remember content. Does it matter that you won't know what happened next or if the person who presented was able to move things on? If you still choose to keep a record of the meeting then be aware that you won't actually be able to record what happened since experience is much more about perception, felt sense, conscious and unconscious reactions, attributed meaning and much less about what closed circuit television cameras would have captured.

Note taking in search of meaning

Sometimes supervisors take notes in an attempt to make meaning out of experience, to piece things together and to trace the journey of events that led from A to Z. If meaning making is what motivates you then be careful not to fall into the trap of believing that the more you understand what happened the more helpful you might be. Yes and no. It is just as possible that the more you try to understand the more confused or baffled you might be and the longer the group session lives on as a private session in your head without the group being present in the ensuing weeks.

Unleashing your inner saboteur

Beware that your notes do not unleash your inner saboteur which destabilizes you and flushes out any shred of confidence and ability you previously had. Consider also whether your notes support or contradict your espoused supervisory style: if you claim to be facilitating groups in a cooperative style (see Note 13) why do your notes place so much responsibility for what happened on you? Conversely if you consider yourself to be a values based supervisor (Note 24) why do your notes privilege your voice and understanding over the inaudible and un-elicited post-session voices of group members? Note taking after sessions, their inherent underlying assumptions, content and purpose, is one of the most acute ways of unearthing the who, what and how of supervision (Note 15) and of holding yourself accountable and in check.

Resonance or Relevance

If you *do* decide to take notes after group supervision, then I suggest you follow Nancy Kline's lead and prioritize issues of resonance (what ignites) over issues of relevance (detailed analysis). The following questions are offered in that vein to help you track your inner growth, freedom and identity:

> What were my pre-transferences before the session began? Were any of them played out in the session? What echoes did the group carry from my family of origin? Who did I align with (matches/pairing/twinning)? Who did I recruit to assist me when things got tough (scratches, rescuers)? How did I host the group reflexive conversation? What was my contribution to creating an environment conducive to reflection? How did I foster trust, collaboration, cooperation, creativity, compassion? Did I in any way contribute to competition, collusion, cynicism? How did I harness the group's wisdom in the service of learning?

This is not a checklist to work through, but rather an invitation to follow the resounding resonance or reverberations with which you are left following any given group session.

If you choose to take notes be free. Note taking does not have to be verbal or committed to paper. You may prefer to respond in the body, or by drawing, or through musical improvisation. You might like to sift through a pack of image cards or create a small world installation which externalises your internalised experience. And you might like to take your resonances - and photos of your installations or drawings - to supervision on supervision. Doing so neatly aligns your self-care with your core purpose in caring for others.

Keeping it simple

Note taking isn't the only way of reviewing or keeping track of sessions. Experiment with non-verbal reviews of your growth as a supervisor. And take care not to rehearse the session multiple times in the space between group meetings without the participants present.

Checking my assumptions

Who am I to assume
that life stands still
outside of the group being together
As though life were lived in some great vacuum
between group sessions
That my possibly flawed perception
of where we arrived together
will be the point to which we return?
Taking no account that each participant
in this diverse group
has continued to practice their myriad skills
Why would I want to encapsulate a moment in time
even one that seemed to afford great insight
or that demanded renewed curiosity
The beauty of supervision
is the in the moment discovery
that has the potential to change our future practice
by sharpening our skills at the point of delivery
It is a beauty that finds traction
not in documentation
but in continued practice.

Note 43 Supervision on Supervision

'Care giving often calls us to lean into love we didn't know possible.'
Tia Walker [1]

When you think of accessing supervision for the supervision groups you facilitate first notice what comes to mind. Would you automatically think of going to individual supervision or to group supervision? And what does your choice indicate about your underlying beliefs, values and needs about either?

When experienced supervisors add group supervision into their working portfolios they can find themselves back in the novice or apprentice stage of practitioner development (See Note 12) and seek out authoritative supervision from someone with significantly more group experience than they currently have. Sitting at the feet of the expert they benefit from having their formative, restorative and performative needs met: they seek coaching and skills development; they value admitting mistakes and the opportunity to recover lost confidence; they may also appreciate hints and tips on supervising more effectively.

Those who supervise beginning supervisors need to pay particular attention lest they deskill them, feed their sense of inadequacy and undermine their autonomy as practitioners. Normative supervision may be your default seat on the five seater sofa (Note 14) but may not be what the supervisor in training needs. Similarly supervisors who default to the transformative dimension of supervision may make it well-nigh impossible for beginning group supervisors to have their formative 'need to know' needs met. Neither holding supervisees back nor pushing them forward gives them sufficient security to learn in the current moment.

Be aware what you *think* you are seeking in supervision on supervision and of what the group might be *directing* you to seek. It's one thing to consciously ask your supervisor to play the expert, to diagnose the problem and prescribe a course of action which you intend to follow. It is quite another to unconsciously replay with your supervisor a dynamic that the group rehearses with you. Having a supervisor who can work with the whole gamut of transference, countertransference, parallel process, somatization and projection in the supervisory space will be very helpful for your own professional development and confidence.

Who could supervise your work?

Given the dearth of qualified and experienced cross-professional supervisors who work from a soul, role and context framework it would be easy to think of asking one of your supervision trainers to supervise the group work you do. This has the advantage that you already know and probably trust each other, have a good rapport and can deepen course learning through the ongoing relationship. The pitfalls include never quite making the transition from trainer/student to a peer/peer relationship and of becoming further entrenched in the trainer's conceptual frameworks, modalities and pet theories at the risk of loss of breadth and diversity with a new supervisor.

If you do choose to look for someone outside your training network you may have more choice over the supervisory approach which suits you best. The disadvantages are that your practice narrows again from the cross-professional breadth to a disciplinary paradigm. ('Although I supervise across a range of disciplines I do so from a psychotherapeutic paradigm therefore I am going to seek out a psychotherapist to supervise my group supervision work.')

Another option is to seek peer supervision with a colleague or colleagues. Pre-existent collegial relationships are likely to mean that you have a reasonable sense of each other and possibly also of each other's working context. The downside however is the high risk of collusion and avoidance and of prioritizing the social relationship over the wellbeing of those in each other's care.

Supervision within a community of practice mitigates against some (though not all) of the risks associated with peer supervision. As a form of consultative supervision, recurring themes or patterns in your work with groups could be aired, resources shared and live supervision offered. (The Institute of Pastoral Supervision and Reflective Practice offers online cross-professional group supervision within an international community of practitioners: more details from training @ipsrp.org.uk)

Keeping it simple

In finding a Supervisor for your Group Supervision work, consider what would best help you to continue to develop as a supervisor. Is it in a group – with peer support and/or collegiality or might it be a cross professional supervisor who is willing to emerge from their disciplinary paradigm to create space to learn with you in attending to your ongoing development. Notice your thoughts and feelings about considering a new start. These will be echoed in those contemplating working with you.

Being and doing

When I join a group
bringing my practice, my curiosity, and myself
What will play out as I seek to reflect
What will I mirror of the reflection I've fostered
What will be transformed
And what will be transmitted
Who will help me see
the self that practices
Both when I welcome insight and when I resist?
Who will meet me in my vulnerability
And who will challenge me in my confidence
And how might the resonance I meet
find some resolution in a space of mutual encounter.

A sleeping tiger

The outward smoke and flame
conceals a heart that contains an energy
a white hot heat that fuels and sustains
And, even when the flames die down
and the smoke disperses
the smouldering ash lies ready
to be coaxed into new life
to be fanned into flame
by a breath of wind
or a new source of fuel
that provides feeding
for the sleeping tiger
that remains crouched in our midst.

'Sometimes the embers are better than the campfire'
Stephen King[2]

Afterword

Michael & Liz have given wholeheartedly, so we can learn wholeheartedly the heart of supervision, the realness it can offer those who are bold and willing to learn about themselves, but also bold and willing enough to grow and develop in their care for the other who is often only afforded the time of those directly helping.

Michael brings such a warmth and compassion as he shares. He encourages the reader, the supervisor to learn and practice 'being' in supervision, demonstrating the true depth of experience and learning it brings. I've learnt more and more deeply not only strategies, but ways of being myself to allow space for my supervisees and the people they represent.

Liz's poetry is shared straight from the heart, and allows the reader to pause and dig ever more deeply into their own reflexivity, to bring greater capacity to pause and be, to reflect and to connect with themselves in order to grow and be present for the other.

I am so grateful for this book. As I read, it's like I am in supervision with Michael. Each Note allowing pause, ponder and reflection. Each Note & 'Keeping it simple' section, allowing me to learn some more. I know this book will be both experiential and also a wonderfully helpful support to all supervisors embarking on group supervision. Michael takes the reader on a journey from concepts to participants to practice, all of which are needed if we are to comprehensively provide a space for people to reflect and be reflective.

I am truly honoured to share these few words about two wonderful people who embody the heart and soul of supervision and who have truly shared of themselves to allow us all to grow and develop.

Thank you Michael and Liz.

Dr Rebecca Loundar
Associate Professor
Alphacrucis University College
Australia

References

Note 1 Supervision in a Nutshell

1. Sheila Ryan (2004) *Vital Practice: Stories from the Healing Arts The Homeopathic and Supervisory Way*, Portland, UK: Sea Change, 106.
2. See Michael Paterson (2020) *Between a Rock and a Hard Place* for wider discussion of developing understandings of the term 'supervision', 9-20.
3. For a fuller discussion see Paterson (2020) 9-20.
4. Donald Schon (1985) *The Reflective Practitioner: How professionals think in action*. London: Temple Smith.

Note 2 Supervising Across the Professions

1. Brigid Proctor commenting on Michael Carroll's research in Brigid Proctor (2008) *Group Supervision: A Guide to Creative Practice* (2nd Edition) London: Sage, 15.
2. Janine Bernard and Rodney Goodyear, *Fundamentals of clinical supervision* (4th Edition) Boston: Pearson Allyn & Bacon, 244. The 6th edition was published in 2019.
3. Michael Carroll's work spans counselling, coaching, organizational consultancy and supervision.
4. *Droichead Journal of the Supervisors Association of Ireland*, launched in 2017 is the only Cross-Professional Supervision Journal in the English speaking world. It is available from the Supervisors of Ireland https://saivision.ie/ Accessed 12 October 2022.

Note 3 When is Supervision not Supervision

1. Clive Staple Lewis (1955) *The Magicians' Nephew,* London: The Bodley Head.
2. Helena Hargaden writes: 'The supervisor is responsible for not allowing herself to be in a confluence of opinion with the group, but to keep a part of her mind on the responsibility to the client.' Helena Hargaden (2016) *The Art of Relational Supervision: Clinical Implications of the use of Self in Group Supervision*, London: Routledge, 146.

Note 4 Supervision begins in Community

1. Stanley Hauerwas, 'A Story-Formed Community: Reflections on "Watership Down" (1981)', reprinted in John Berkman and Michael Cartwright (eds.) (2001) *The Hauerwas Reader*, Durham and London: Duke University Press, 171–99.
2. Gaie Houston (1993) *The Red Book of Groups and How to lead them better,* Aylsham: Rochester Foundation; Brigid Proctor (2008) *Group Supervision: A Guide to Creative Practice* (2nd Edition) London: Sage.
3. Personal Protective Equipment.
4. Margaret Thatcher, UK Prime Minister 1979–1990, famously quipped 'Society? There is no such thing as society'. Cited in Margaret Thatcher (1987) 'Interview for "Woman's Own" ("No Such Thing as Society")' in *Margaret Thatcher: Speeches, Interviews and Other Statements.* London: Margaret Thatcher Foundation.
5. Karine Polwart Scottish songwriter observing how a flock of migrating geese take up different positions to buffer the storm and get the whole skein through long flights battling with the elements.
6. 'It was the best of times, it was the worst of times, it was the age of wisdom, it was the age of foolishness, it was the epoch of belief, it was the epoch of incredulity, it was the season of light, it was the season of darkness, it was the spring of hope, it was the winter of despair.' Charles Dickens, *A Tale of Two Cities.*

7. John Whittington, (2020) Systemic Coaching and Constellations, (3rd Edition) London: Kogan Page, 278.
8. John Whittington (2020) 54.

Note 5 Who you are is Why you Supervise

1. Keemar Keemar (2020) Presentation at ISN Conference 'Supervision as Autobiography'. 3 July cited in Birch, J. (2022) *Coaching Supervision Groups: Resourcing Practitioners*, London: Routledge, 199.
2. Edna Murdoch and Jackie Arnold (2013) *Full Spectrum Supervision: Who you are is how you Supervise*, St Alban: Panoma Press.
3. Normative, formative and restorative tasks of supervision see Francesca Inskipp and Brigid Proctor (1988, 1993) *The Art, Craft and Tasks of Counselling Supervision, Part 1: Making the most of Supervision* (1st Edition) Twickenham: Cascade Publications.
4. Originally termed the 6 modes, later recast as the 7 eyes, Hawkins and Shohet;s work has been the main supervision reference point in the English speaking world. See Hawkins and McMahon, (2020) *Supervising in the Helping professions*, (5th Edition) London: OUP, 85–114.
5. Steve Page and Val Wosket (1994) *Supervising the Counsellor. A Cyclical Model*, London: Routledge.
6. 'Supervision may have a key role to play in the reconstruction of the authentic professional self. The supervision issues of mature, experienced practitioners are also their life issues.' Page and Wosket (1994) 229.
7. Carl Jung, father of depth psychology; Hans Kung, one of the great Roman Catholic theologians of the 20th century; Michael Carroll supervisor extraordinaire.
8. John Whittington (2020) 50.

Note 6 Family Echoes in Groups

1. Bert Hellinger, Gunthard Weber; Hunter Beaumont (1998) *Love's Hidden*

Symmetry: What Makes Love Work in Relationships, Brand: Zeig, Tucker Theisen.

2. Wilfred Bion refers to this as 'pairing' in Wilfrid Bion, (1961). *Experiences in Groups*, London: Tavistock, 62.
3. John Whittington, (2020) 51.
4. John Whittington (2020) 281.

Note 7 Integrated and Unresolved Family Echoes in Groups

1. Antonio Damasio (1999) *The Feeling of What Happens: Body and Emotion in the Making of Consciousness*, New York: Harcourt Brace.
2. Unless provoked by unconscious and homeless dynamics in the material being explored. See Note 31 'Dynamics'.
3. Cf Stephen Karpman, (1968),'Fairy tales and script drama analysis', *Transactional Analysis Bulletin* 7 (26) 39-43. See also Note 31 'Dynamics'.
4. On role repertoire see Anna Chesner and Lia Zografou (2013) *Creative Supervision Across Modalities*, London: Jessica Kingsley 43-46.

Note 8 The Effective Group Supervisor

1. Brian Patten, *Selected Poems*, 2007.
2. Marie-Louise Ögren, Siv Boalt Boëthius, and Eva Sundin (2014), 'Challenges and Possibilities in Group Supervision' in C. Edward Watkins, Jr. and Derek L. Milne (2014) *The Wiley International Handbook of Clinical Supervision*, 1st Edition, 654.
3. 'If you'd like to move forward with fluency and clarity, look back first. From that will come clarity, insight and then release and resource.' Whittington (2020) 282.
4. Paul Ricoeur (1970) *Freud and Philosophy: An Essay on Interpretation.* New Haven: Yale University Press.
5. 'If you want to use your past challenges as a source of strength and resource they will need to be brought into your compassionate conscious awareness.' Whittington (2020) 6.

6. John Whittington (2020) 7.

Note 9 Stages of Group Life

1. Gaie Houston cited in Brigid Proctor (2008) 17.
2. Bruce Wayne Tuckman (1965) 'Developmental sequences in small groups', *Psychological Bulletin* 63 (6): 384-99. Revised to include 'mourning' (sometimes 'adjourning'). See Bruce Wayne and Mary Ann Jensen (1977) 'Stages of small-group development revised', *Group and Organization Management* 2 (4): 419-427. Tuckman is not without his critiques. Linda Yael Shiller (1997) argues that stages of group development may be influenced by gender and that in a 'women-only group' the three middle stages are 'establishing a relational base; mutuality and interpersonal empathy and challenge and change'. Linda Yael Schiller (1997) 'Rethinking stages of development in women's groups: Implications for practice', *Social Work with Groups* 20 (3); 3-19.
3. William C. Schutz (1973) *Elements of Encounter*, Big Sur, CA: Joy Press.
4. Wilfrid Bion (1961) *Experience in Groups* London: Tavistock
5. Bion (1961) argues that in every group, two groups are actually present: the work group, and the basic assumption group. Those in the work group are focused on the primary task of the group. The 'basic assumption group' is driven by the underlying – behind the scenes – assumptions within the group which fall into three modes: dependency, fight-flight, and pairing.

Note 10 Difference and Diversity in Groups

1. Michael Carroll and Margaret Tholstrup (2001) *Integrative Approaches to Supervision* London: Jessica Kingsley, 19.
2. David Clutterbuck, Carol Whitaker and Michelle Lucas (2016) *Coaching Supervision: A Practical Guide for Supervisees*, London: Routledge, 183.

Note 11 An Overview of Group Supervision

1. Cf Rodney Goodyear and M. Nelson (1997) 'The major formats of psychotherapy supervision' in E. Watkins (Eds.), *Handbook of Psychotherapy Supervision*, 11–27. New York: John Wiley & Sons.
2. In 1962 *Time* magazine printed a version of the quotation credited to Einstein in 'A Letter From The Publisher.'
3. Fuller discussion in Note 1 'Supervision in a Nutshell'.
4. Fuller discussion in Note 19 'Role of the Supervisor'.
5. Fuller discussion in Note 30 'Contracting with The Group'.
6. Fuller discussion in Note 5 'Who you are is why you Supervise'; Note 6 'Family Echoes in Groups'.
7. See Note 6 'Family Echoes in Groups'.
8. Wilfrid Bion (1961).
9. Cf Patrick Lencioni's 'Five Dysfunctions of a Team' in which the 'we' (commitment) is the middle of a five tiered pyramid with trust and conflict below and accountability and results above. Patrick Lencioni (2002) *The Five Dysfunctions of a Team*, San Francisco: Jossey-Bass. In my adaptation of Lencioni, I have modified his second tier 'conflict' to 'difference' since experience has taught that when differences are acknowledged and embraced (rather than swept under the carpet) the likelihood of conflict arising is reduced
10. See Note 31 on dynamics arising within a group and from the material being explored and Note 34 'Reviewing the Group's life'.
11. See Note 27 'Preparing to meet a Group for the First Time'.

Note 12 Attuning to Supervisees' Needs

1. Cal D. Stoltenberg and Ursula Delworth (1987) *Supervising Counselors and Therapists: A Developmental Approach.* San Francisco, CA: Jossey-Bass; Cal D. Stoltenberg and Brian W. McNeill (2010) *IDM Supervision: An Integrative Developmental model for supervising counsellors and therapists.* San Francisco, CA: Jossey-Bass; Peter Hawkins and Aisling McMahon,

(2020).

Note 13 Group Styles

1. Elizabeth Holloway & Rebecca Johnston (1985) 'Group supervision: Widely practiced but poorly understood' *Counselor Education and Supervision,* 24 (4), 332–340. See too Loreto Prieto (1996) 'Group supervision: Still widely practiced but poorly understood' *Counselor Education and Supervision,* 35 (4), 295–307.
2. Adapted from the typologies of Brigid Proctor and Eric Berne. See too Liz Beddoe and Allyson Davys (2016) *Challenges in Professional Supervision: Current Themes and Models for Practice*, London: Jessica Kingsley, 130-31.
3. Brigid Proctor (2008) 31-49.
4. Eric Berne in Brigid Proctor (2008) 32.
5. Liz Beddoe and Allyson Davys (2016) 133.

Note 14 The Tasks of Group Supervision

1. Renee Swope is an American motivational speaker and blogger. https://reneeswope.com/ Accessed 28 September 2022
2. Francesca Inskipp and Brigid Proctor (1988, 1993). Since then Alfred Kadushin, and Daniel Harkness have adapted their framework to denote the Administrative, Educational, and Supportive tasks of supervision. See Alfred Kadushin, and Daniel Harkness (2002) *Supervision in Social Work.* New York, NY: Columbia University Press.
3. Michael Carroll (2008) 'Supervision and Transformational Learning' *Psychotherapy in Australia* 14 (3), 38-45, 43.
4. cf Bobby Moore Foreword.

Note 15 Who is Group Supervision For?

1. David Paré (2016) 'Creating a Space for Acknowledgment and Generativity in Reflective Group Supervision' *Family Process,* 55 (2), 270-86.

2. Audre Lorde (1984) *Sister Outsider: Essays and Speeches.* Ed. Berkeley, CA: Crossing Press.
3. Patrick Lencioni (2002) names the lack of commitment in groups as 'feigned buy in' which results in ambiguity throughout the system.
4. Sociometry literally means the metrics of associations or relationships.

Note 16 What issues do participants bring?

1. Mick O'Keeffe and James Forrest (2014) 'Facilitated group supervision: Harnessing the power of peers' *Journal of Paediatrics and Child Health* 50, 944.
2. Gillie Bolton and Russell Delderfield (2018) *Reflective Practice: Writing and Professional Development* 5th edition, London: Sage, xvi.
3. Michael Carroll (2007) 'One More Time: What is Supervision?', *Psychotherapy in Australia* 13(3), 34–40.
4. Allan Brown and Ian Bourne (1996) *The Social Work Supervisor,* Buckingham, OUP, 145.
5. The 'Inner Wise Guide' supervisory modality is outlined in Michael Paterson and Liz Crumlish (2021) *Pastoral Supervision: Creativity in Action*, Edinburgh: IPSRP, 173.
6. 'Clean language' in supervision is outlined in Paterson and Crumlish (2021) 179–81.

Note 17 How many people make a group?

1. http://changingminds.org/explanations/groups/minimum_group_siz e.htm Accessed 28 September 2022.
2. See Note 13 'Group Styles'.
3. Steve Page and Val Wosket (1994).*al Model,* London: Routledge.
4. The authors run in-person and online creative supervision groups for practitioners and for supervisors. If you would like to experience creative supervision within an international community of practice contact training@ipsrp.org.uk

Note 18 Benefits and Challenges of Group Supervision

1. Timothy Radcliffe O.P. *The Tablet Blog*, 21 Sep 2021.
2. Brigid Proctor (2008) xvi.
3. Marie-Louise Ögren et al. (2014) 649.
4. Marie-LouiseÖgren et al (2014) 648.
5. Tamara Sussman, Marian Bogo and Judith Globerman (2007) 'Field instructor competence in group supervision: Establishing trust through managing group dynamics', *The Clinical Supervisor*, 26 (1/2): 61–80.
6. See fuller discussion in Note 10 'Difference and Diversity'.
7. Helena Hargaden (2016), 135.

Note 19 The Role of the Group Supervisor

1. Sheila Ryan (2004) 79-80.
2. I have been unable to identify the source of this insight.
3. Authoritative, participative, cooperative, peer are forms of group supervision according to Brigid Proctor's typology, see Note 13 'Group Styles'.
4. Brigid Proctor (2008) writes 'being authoritative without being authoritarian can be quite a difficult balance to strike both for the naturally bossy and the naturally timid' 73.
5. John Adair (1984) *Action Centred Leadership* London: McGrawHill. According to John Adair effective leaders must 'achieve the task, build and maintain the team and develop the individual'.

Note 20 The Role of Group Supervisees

1. Allan Brown private correspondence. Used with permission.

Note 21 Structuring Group Time

1. Cited in Geoffrey C Ward and Ken Burns (2000) *Jazz: a history of America's*

music, New York: Alfred A. Knopf.

2. For a fuller discussion of the 'Sat Nav' approach to structuring supervision sessions see Michael Paterson (2020) *Between a Rock and a Hard Place: Pastoral Supervision Revisited and Revisioned* Edinburgh: IPSRP, 55-77. For creative modalities which can be used at each stage of the Sat Nav see Michael Paterson and Liz Crumlish (2021) *Pastoral Supervision: Creativity in Action*, Edinburgh: IPSRP or the Australian edition of the same book which is entitled *Creative Pastoral Supervision.* Aisling Vorster is preparing a toolkit for creative online and digital supervision to be ready in 2023. Contact Aisling on mail@aislingvorster.co.uk to register your interest and for advance purchase.
3. The use of chairs, a form of role work is outlined more fully in Michael Paterson and Liz Crumlish (2021).

Note 22 Supervising Teams

1. David Paré (2016) 270.
2. Allyson Davys and Liz Beddoe (2010) *Best Practice in Professional Supervision: A Guide for the Helping Professions*, London: Jessica Kingsley, 82.
3. Steve Page and Val Wosket (1994), 60.
4. Peter Hawkins and Aisling McMahon, (2020) 5.

Note 23 Peer Supervision

1. John Dewey (1933), *How we Think*, Buffalo NY: Prometheus (originally published 1910).
2. Leonard Cohen, 'Sisters of Mercy'.
3. 'A child who takes care of a parent often forges a lifelong pattern of over extension and creates a blueprint for habitually feeling overwhelmed.' Mark Wolynn in Whittington (2020) 284.
4. Sheila Ryan (2004) 85.

Note 24 Supervising Organizations

1. Peter Hawkins and Robin Shohet (2012) *Supervision in the Helping Professions* (4th Edition) 237.
2. Michael Carroll and Margaret Tholstrup (2001) 50. For a fuller discussion of supervision in organizations see Eamonn Casey (2017) 'Obstacles to effective practice in cross-professional supervision when working with organisations', *Droichead Journal of the Supervisors Association of Ireland*, 1, 44-47. See too Ger Holton (2019) 'Practice Research Corner unnamed piece 'Wave-makers: A spotlight on supervision of managers' in *Droichead Journal of the Supervisors Association of Ireland*, 2, 19-22.
3. For more on Values Based Reflective Practice (VBRP) see Michael Paterson and Ewan Kelly (2013) 'Reflective Practice- A Method Developed in Scotland for Spiritual Care Practitioners' *Practical Theology 6.1.*
4. Paul Ricoeur (1975), 'Biblical Hermeneutics' *Semeia* (4) 29–145. Ricoeur's schema has been popularised by Walter Brueggemann in his 1980 publication, 'Psalms and the Life of Faith: A suggested Typology' reprinted in Patrick Miller (1995), *Psalms and the Life of Faith*, Minneapolis, MN: Augsburg Press.
5. Audre Lorde (1984).

Note 26 First Meeting with the Group

1. Vikki Reynolds (2014) 'Centering Ethics in Group Supervision: Fostering cultures of Critique and Structuring Safety' *International Journal of Narrative Therapy and Community Work*, 1, 7.
2. Vikki Reynolds (2014) 1, 7.

Note 27 Preparing to Meet a Group for the First Time

1. Ram Dass and Paul Gorman (1985) *How can I help? Stories and Reflections on Service*, London: Rider, 191.
2. There is some truth in the old saying 'you only get the clients you

deserve'. In my experience supervisees often present with issues that we ourselves need to attend to: poor interpersonal relationships at work; dips in professional confidence; loss of joy at work; ethical dilemmas etc.. Reflecting on what is brought our way can sometimes reveal areas for our own - out of session - explorations.

Note 28 Preparing Supervisees for their First Session

1. Allan Brown and Ian Bourne (1996) *The Social Work Supervisor*. Buckingham: Open University Press, 144.
2. Michael Carroll cited in Rachel Tribe and Jean Morrissey ed (2004) *Handbook of Professional and Ethical Practice for Psychologists, Counsellors and Psychotherapists*, Brunner-Routledge, 93-4.

Note 29 Boundaries

1. Vikki Reynolds (2014) 7.
2. Vikki Reynolds (2014) 8.
3. Vikki Reynolds (2014) 8.
4. Vikki Reynolds (2014) 8.
5. Mary Creanor (2014) *Getting the Best out of Supervision in Counselling and Psychotherapy: A Guide for the Supervisee*, London: Sage, 59.
6. For fuller discussion see Stephen Power (2007) 'Boundaries and responsibilities in clinical supervision' in John Driscoll (ed.) *Practicing Clinical Supervision* (2nd Edition) Edinburgh: Baillière Tindall/Elsevier, 53-71.

Note 31 Dynamics in Group Supervision

1. Cited in Michael Carroll and Margaret Tholstrup (2001) 19.
2. Cited in Penny Henderson, Jim Holloway and Anthea Millar (2014) *Practical Supervision: How to become a Supervisor for the Helping Professions*, London: Jessica Kingsley, 32.
3. I am indebted to Helena Hargaden (2016) for providing me with words

for something I learned from experience.

4. These and many other creative modalities are expounded in Michael Paterson and Liz Crumlish (2021) *Pastoral Supervision: Creativity in Action*, Edinburgh: IPSRP. The Australian edition of the same book is entitled *Creative Pastoral Supervision*.
5. Marie-Louise Ögren et al (2014) 654.
6. Marie-Louise Ögren et al (2014) 649.
7. Cf Helena Hargaden (2016) 79.
8. The American educationalist J. Parker Palmer holds that learning groups have three characteristics: Boundaries, openness and hospitality. J. Parker Palmer (1993) *To Know as We are Known: A Spirituality of Education*, San Francisco: Harper, 71-5.
9. Paul Greenhalgh (2000) *Emotional growth and learning*, London: Routledge, 192.

Note 32 Characters in Groups

1. John Towler (2001) 'Which Sub-personality is supervising today?' in Michael Carroll and Margaret Tholstrup (2001) 174-182.

Note 33 Help! I'm Stuck!

1. See John Whittington, (2020) 234-35.
2. See the Secret language of systems in John Whittington, (2020) 138-42.

Note 34 Reviewing the Life of a Group

1. See Note 6 'Family Echoes in Groups'.
2. See Note 9 'Stages of Group Life'.
3. Cited in Penny Henderson et al. (2014) 32.
4. See Note 37 'Giving and Receiving'.
5. See Note 39 'Group Ethos'.
6. Cited in Bobby Moore, (2017) 167.

Note 35 Endings in Groups

1. Brigid Proctor (2008) 99.
2. Peter Hawkins and Robin Shohet, Eye 6.
3. For a more extensive exploration of endings in supervision see Jane Leach and Michael Paterson (2015) *Pastoral Supervision: A Handbook* London: SCM, 243-59.

Note 36 Resonance over Relevance

1. Carol Perry (2014) *Waiting for Our Souls to Catch Up: Reason, Ritual and Faith in Our Fallow Time*, Los Angeles: Asahina and Wallace.
2. Nancy Kline (2020).
3. It is a form of 'listening to ignite' Nancy Kline, (2019).

Note 37 On Giving and Receiving

1. Sheila Ryan (2004) 97.
2. From the untitled poem by Beth Strano.

Note 38 The Nine Beats

1. Megan McKenna (1999) *Blessings and Woes: The Beatitudes and the Sermon on the Plain in the Gospel of Luke,* New York: Orbis Books 22-23.
2. Based on Nine Beats Collective / Mark Scandrette (2017), *Ninefold Path Notebook*, 82, published by Lifewords. Used with permission.

Note 39 Group Ethos

1. Louie Gardiner (2022) 'Moving Bodies' in Jo Birch (2022) *Coaching Supervision Groups: Resourcing Practitioners*, London: Routledge 106.

Note 40 Supervising Barefoot

1. I am grateful to my good friend and colleague Les Underwood for the term 'Barefoot Supervisor', the title of his outstanding workshop at the Australia and New Zealand Association for Clinical Pastoral Education (ANZACPE) Conference 2022.
2. Macrina Wiedekehr osb (1991) *Seasons of Your Heart* New York: Harper-One.
3. Vikki Reynolds (2014) 6.
4. Michael Foucault cited in Vikki Reynolds (204) 6.

Note 41 Self-Care for Supervisors

1. Helena Hargaden (2016) 140.
2. For a fuller exploration of self-care in supervision see Jack Finnegan (2017) 'Self-Care: Style and Substance', *Droichead Journal of the Supervisors Association of Ireland*, 1, 48-56.
3. From the song 'This is Me' written by Justin Paul and Benj Pasek. © Sony/ATV Music Publishing LLC, Kobalt Music Publishing Ltd. featured in the film *The Greatest Showman*.
4. Caroline Schuck and Jane Wood (2011) offer similar exercises for arriving in the room in *Inspiring Creative Supervision*, London: Jessica Kingsley, 157-69.

Note 42 Reflecting Afterwards

1. Finley Peter Dunne (1898). *Mr. Dooley in Peace and in War*. Small, Maynard & Co.

Note 43 Supervision on Supervision

1. Tia Walker (2019) *Caregiver Journal: A comprehensive medical and health record log to stay organized and keep track of your patients,* Independent.

Bibliography

Adair, J. (1984) *Action Centred Leadership* London: McGraw-Hill.

Beddoe, L. and Davys. A. (2016) *Challenges in Professional Supervision: Current Themes and Models for Practice*, London: Jessica Kingsley.

Benefiel, M. and Holton, G. (2010) *The Soul of Supervision: Integrating Practice and Theory*, New York: Morehouse.

Bernard, J. and Goodyear, R. (2019) *Fundamentals of clinical supervision* (6th Edition) Boston: Pearson Allyn & Bacon.

Bion, W. (1961). *Experiences in Groups*, London: Tavistock.

Birch, J. (2022) *Coaching Supervision Groups: Resourcing Practitioners*, London: Routledge.

Bolton, G. (2018), *Reflective Practice: Writing and Professional Development*, (5th Edition) London: Sage.

Brown, A. and Bourne, I. (1996) *The Social Work Supervisor*, Buckingham, OUP.

Brueggemann, W. (1980) 'Psalms and the Life of Faith: A suggested Typology' reprinted in Patrick Miller ed. (1995), *Psalms and the Life of Faith*, Minneapolis, MN: Augsburg Press.

Carroll, M. (2007) 'One more time: what is supervision?' *Psychotherapy in Australia,* 13(3), 34-40.

Carroll, M. (2008) 'Supervision and Transformational Learning' *Psychotherapy in Australia* 14(3), 38-45.

Carroll, M. (2009). 'From mindless to mindful practice: On learning reflection in supervision.' *Psychotherapy in Australia*, 15(4), 38-49.

Carroll, M. and Tholstrup, M. (2001) *Integrative Approaches to Supervision* London: Jessica Kingsley.

Casey, E. (2017) 'Obstacles to effective practice in cross-professional supervision when working with organisations', *Droichead Journal of the Supervisors Association of Ireland*, 1, 44-47.

Chesner, A. and Hahn, H. (2001) *Creative Advances in Groupwork*, London: Jessica Kingsley.

Chesner, A. and Zografou, L. (2013) *Creative Supervision Across Modalities*, London: Jessica Kingsley.

Clutterbuck, D., Whitaker, D. and Lucas, M. (2016) *Coaching Supervision: A Practical Guide for Supervisees*, London: Routledge.

Creanor, M. (2014) *Getting the Best out of Supervision in Counselling and Psychotherapy: A Guide for the Supervisee*, London: Sage

Damasio, A. (1999) *The Feeling of What Happens: Body and Emotion in the Making of Consciousness*, New York: Harcourt Brace.

Davys, A. and Beddoe, L. (2010) *Best Practice in Professional Supervision: A Guide for the Helping Professions*, London: Jessica Kingsley.

Finnegan, J. (2017) 'Self-Care: Style and Substance', *Droichead Journal of the Supervisors Association of Ireland*, 1, 48-56.

Gardiner, L. (2022) 'Moving Bodies' in Jo Birch (2022) *Coaching Supervision Groups: Resourcing Practitioners*, London: Routledge.

Goodyear, R. and Nelson, M. (1997) 'The major formats of psychotherapy supervision' in E. Watkins (Ed.), *Handbook of psychotherapy supervision*, New York: John Wiley & Sons, 11–27.

Hargaden, H. (2016) *The Art of Relational Supervision: Clinical Implications of the use of Self in Group Supervision*, London: Routledge.

Hauerwas, S. (1981) 'A Story-Formed Community: Reflections on "Watership Down" (1981)', reprinted in John Berkman and Michael Cartwright (eds.) (2001) *The Hauerwas Reader*, Durham and London: Duke University Press.

Hawkins, P. and McMahon, A. (2020) *Supervising in the Helping professions*, (5th Edition) London: OUP.

Hawkins, P. and Shohet, R. (2012) *Supervision in the Helping Professions* (4th Edition), Milton Keynes: OUP.

Hawkins, P. and Smith, N. (2013) *Coaching, Mentoring And Organizational Consultancy: Supervision, Skills And Development.* London: McGraw-Hill.

Hellinger, B., Weber, G. and Beaumont, H. (1998) *Love's Hidden Symmetry: What Makes Love Work in Relationships,* Brand: Zeig, Tucker Theisen.

Henderson, P., Holloway, J. and Millar, A. (2014) *Practical Supervision: How to become a Supervisor for the Helping Professions*, London: Jessica Kingsley.

Holton, G. (2017) 'Cross-Professional Supervision: A Bridge Across Professions', Droichead Journal of the Supervisors Association of Ireland, 1(1) 6-19.

Holton,G. (2019) 'Practice Research Corner unnamed piece 'Wave-makers: A spotlight on supervision of managers' in *Droichead Journal of the Supervisors Association of Ireland*, 2, 19-22.

Holloway, E. L., & Johnston, R. (1985). 'Group supervision: Widely practiced but poorly understood.' *Counselor Education and Supervision, 24(4)*, 332–340.

Houston, G. (1993) *The Red Book of Groups and How to lead them better,* Aylsham: Rochester Foundation.

Inskipp, F. and Proctor, B. (1988, 1993) *The Art, Craft and Tasks of Counselling Supervision, Part 1: Making the most of Supervision* (1st Edition) Twickenham: Cascade Publications.

Kadushin, A. and Harkness, D. (2002). *Supervision in social work.* New York, NY: Columbia University Press.

Karpman, K. (1968),'Fairy tales and script drama analysis', *Transactional Analysis Bulletin* 7:26, 39-43.

Kline, N. (1999) *Time to Think,* London: Cassell.

Kline, N. (2020) *The Promise That Changes Everything: I Won't interrupt You,* London: Penguin.

Lahad, M. (2000) *Creative Supervision*, London: Jessica Kingsley Publishers.

Leach, J. and Paterson, M. (2015) *Pastoral Supervision: A Handbook* (2nd Edition) London: SCM.

Lencioni, P. (2002) *The Five Dysfunctions of a Team,* San Francisco: Jossey-Bass.

Lewis, C.S. (1955) *The Magicians' Nephew,* London: The Bodley Head.

Lorde, A. (1984) *Sister Outsider: Essays and Speeches.* Ed. Berkeley, CA: Crossing Place.

McKenna, M. (1999) *Blessings and Woes: The Beatitudes and the Sermon on the Plain in the Gospel of Luke*, New York: Orbis Books.

Moore, B. (2017) *Reflexive Supervision: A workbook for learning within and across professions,* Independently Published.

Murdoch, E. and Arnold, J. (2013) *Full Spectrum Supervision: Who you are is how you Supervise*, St Alban: Panoma Press.

Nine Beats Collective / Mark Scandrette (2017), *Ninefold Path Notebook*, 82, Lifewords.

Ögren, M.L. and Jonsson, C.O. (2005) 'Group Supervision in Psychotherapy: The Relationship Between Focus, Group Climate, and Perceived Attained Skill', *Journal of Clinical Psychology*, 61(4), 373–388.

Ögren, M.L, Boëthius, S. B. and Sundin, E. (2014), ' Challenges and Possibilities in Group Supervision' in C. Edward Watkins, Jr. and Derek L. Milne eds. (2014) *The Wiley International Handbook of Clinical Supervision* (1st Edition): Oxford: Wiley.

O'Keeffe, M. and Forrest, J. (2014) 'Facilitated group supervision: Harnessing the power of peers' *Journal of Paediatrics and Child Health* 50, 944–948.

Page, S. and Wosket, V. (2001) *Supervising the Counsellor: A Cyclical Model,* London: Routledge.

David Paré (2016) 'Creating a Space for Acknowledgment and Generativity in Reflective Group Supervision' *Family Process*, 55(2), 270-86

Paterson, M. (2020) *Between a Rock and a Hard Place: Pastoral Supervision Revisited and Revisioned* Edinburgh: IPSRP.

Paterson, M. and Crumlish, L. (2021) *Creative Approaches in Pastoral Supervision.* Australian edition of *Pastoral Supervision: Creativity in Action.*

Paterson, M. and Crumlish, L. (2021) *Pastoral Supervision: Creativity in Action*, Edinburgh: IPSRP.

Paterson, M. and Crumlish, L. (2023) *Group Supervision in Practice,* Edinburgh: IPSRP.

Paterson, M. and Kelly, E. (2013) 'Reflective Practice- A Method Developed in Scotland for Spiritual Care Practitioners' *Practical Theology* 6(1), 51-68.

Paterson, M. and Rose, J. (2014) *Enriching Ministry: Pastoral Supervision in Context*, London: SCM.

Perry, C. (2014) *Waiting for Our Souls to Catch Up: Reason, Ritual and Faith in*

Our Fallow Time, Los Angeles: Asahina and Wallace

Piggot-Irvine, E. and Biggs, K. (2020) *Leadership Coaching, Mentoring, Counselling or Supervision: One Way is Not Enough*, Newcastle: Cambridge Scholars Publishing.

Prieto, L. R. (1996) 'Group supervision: Still widely practiced but poorly understood', *Counselor Education and Supervision,* 35(4), 295–307.

Proctor, B. (2008) *Group Supervision: A Guide to Creative Practice* (2nd Edition) London: Sage.

Radcliffe O.P., Fr Timothy, *The Tablet Blog*, 21 Sep 2021.

Ram Dass, R. and Gorman, P. (1985) *How can I help?* London: Rider.

Reynolds, V. (2014) 'Centering Ethics in Group Supervision: Fostering cultures of Critique and Structuring Safety' *International Journal of Narrative Therapy and Community Work*, 1.

Ricoeur, P. (1970) *Freud and Philosophy: An Essay on Interpretation.* New Haven: Yale University Press.

Ricoeur, P. (1975), 'Biblical Hermeneutics' *Semeia* (4) 29–145.

Rose, J. (2013) *Psychology for Pastoral Contexts: A Handbook*, London: SCM.

Ryan, S. (2004) *Vital Practice: Stories from the Healing Arts: The Homeopathic and Supervisory Way*, Portland, UK: Sea Change.

Schiller. L.Y. (1997) 'Rethinking stages of development in women's groups: Implications for practice'. *Social Work with Groups* 20(3), 3-19.

Schon, D. (1985) *The Reflective Practitioner: How professionals think in action.* London: Temple Smith.

Schuck, C. and Wood, J. (2011) *Inspiring Creative Supervision*, London: Jessica Kingsley.

Schutz, W.C. (1973) *Elements of Encounter,* Big Sur, CA: Joy Press.

Stoltenberg, C.D. and Delworth, U. (1987) *Supervising Counselors and Therapists: A Developmental Approach.* San Francisco, CA: Jossey-Bass.

Stoltenberg, C.D. and McNeill, B.W (2010) *IDM Supervision: An Integrative Developmental model for supervising counsellors and therapists.* San Francisco, CA: Jossey-Bass.

Strano, Beth 'Brave Space'.

Sussman, T., Bogo, M. and Globerman, J. (2007) 'Field instructor competence in group supervision: Establishing trust through managing group dynamics', *The Clinical Supervisor*, 26(1/2), 61–80.

Thatcher, M. (1987) 'No Such Thing as Society' in *Margaret Thatcher: Speeches, Interviews and Other Statements.* London: Margaret Thatcher Foundation.

Towler, J. (2001) 'Which Sub-personality is supervising today' in Michael Carroll and Margaret Tholstrup (2001) *Integrative Approaches to Supervision* London: Jessica Kingsley, 174-182.

Tribe, R. and Morrissey, J. Eds (2004) *Handbook of Professional and Ethical Practice for Psychologists, Counsellors and Psychotherapists,* Brunner-Routledge.

Tuckman, B.W. (1965) 'Developmental sequences in small groups', Psychological Bulletin, 63(6), 384-99.

Tuckman, B.W. and Jensen, M.A.C. (1977) 'Stages of small-group development revised', *Group and Organization* management 2(4, 419-427.

Walker, T. (2019) *Caregiver Journal: A comprehensive medical and health record log to stay organized and keep track of your patients,* Independently published.

Weld, N. (2012) *A practical guide to Transformative Supervision for the Helping Professions: Amplifying insight,* London: Jessica Kingsley.

Whittington, J. (2020) *Systemic Coaching and Constellations*, (3rd Edition) London: Kogan Page.

Wiedekehr, M. (1991) *Seasons of Your Heart* New York: HarperOne.

Glossary

Action Methods are deployed in group work and creative supervision. They include embodiment, movement, role work and a range of other methods which rely on action and activity as a primary means of exploring supervisory issues.

Authoritative group supervision. A group led by a named supervisor in which supervisees are typically supervised one after the other in turn. Those not being supervised form the participating audience. Also known as supervision *in* a group.

Bridging. One of the stages in the supervisory Sat Nav where a bridge is built between reflection (in the room) and action (back at work).

Clinical Supervision. method employed in the training and development of professionals in healthcare settings, social work, counselling, etc.. Focuses on the practitioner's identity, skills and theoretical framework by reporting on and shared reflection on their work.

Closing. The final moment in the supervision session when things are wrapping up and people are about to leave.

Collusion. An unacknowledged but not always conscious agreement to turn a blind eye to challenging aspects of group life and/or practice.

Communication by impact. An unconscious process whereby one person communicates what they are experiencing to others through the impact they have upon them.

Containing. A component of hosting through which supervisors holding to the group.

Contemplative Inquiry. Also known as The Three Levels of Seeing: I notice, wonder, I realise. See the Greek of John 20 in the Christian Scriptures.

Contracting. The process of establishing shared agreements for the work of supervision.

Cooperative group supervision. A form of supervision in which the supervisor draws in the group as co-supervisors. Also known as supervision *by* a group.

Counter-transference. A psychoanalytic term describing an unconscious process by which feelings, thoughts and behaviours originating in another context or relationship are stimulated in a care giver by the person or group with whom they are working.

Creative modalities. Ways of working in supervision which focus on less verbal means of communication, (eg art, music, drama) and which draw on the imagination to bring what is unconsciously known into consciousness.

Cross-professional supervision. A term coined by Ger Holton for supervision when the locus of expertise lies not in working in the same field as the supervisee (Uni-professional supervision) but in being skilled in hosting and facilitating reflexive conversations.

Cyclical model. Steve Page and Val Wosket's model of supervision.

Drama Triangle. Stephen Karpman's term which describes the roles we take when confronted with issues that are too hard to face: Victim, Persecutor, Rescuer. See too Empowerment Triangle.

Dynamics. The energies, patterns of interaction, conscious and unconscious influences which impact on group process and group participants.

Dysfunctional group. Patrick Lencioni identifies five characteristics of dysfunctional groups: they lack trust, are unable to work with their differences, cannot find common agreement, are unaccountable and unable to achieve their purpose.

Eliciting. The second stage in the supervisory Sat Nav in which material is brought for exploration.

Embodiment. The recognition that the body is wise and highly informative in supervision.

Empathy. Drawing alongside someone else's feelings or experience.

Empowerment Triangle. As the flip side of the Drama Triangle it describes the alternative roles of being Vulnerable, Potent and Responsive.

Enactment. What supervisees do after supervision with the insights they have found in the session.

Exploring in supervision. The space between presentation of an issue and the response or enactment which follows. This constitutes the core task to which the majority of time is allotted.

Five seater sofa. Michael Paterson's name for the enlargement of the three legged stool to include the performative and transformative tasks.

Focusing. Once an issue has been brought into the supervisory space, focusing is the name given to the distillation process which drills deeper into it.

Formative. A term which derives from Inskipp and Proctor's three legged stool in which the focus is on helping the supervisee grow and develop as a practitioner.

Forming. The first stage in Tuckman's life cycle of a group.

Functional model of supervision. An approach to supervision which seeks to outline the main tasks of the discipline, for example Inskipp & Procter's, normative, formative, restorative model, or Michael Carroll's seven tasks of supervision.

Functional groups. According to Patrick Lencioni functional groups are characterised by trust, ability to tolerate difference, shared commitment, accountability and results.

Ground rules. The behaviour and attitudes co-created by groups which govern the supervisory time and process.

Hosting. The core task of the supervisor, to host a reflexive conversation. Hospitality trumps everything in supervision.

Image cards. Collections of art work, postcards or photographs which can be used in supervision.

Imagining in supervision. The space for considering options and alternatives when exploring a supervisory issue.

Insight. Amplified vision is the whole purpose of supervision.

Installation. The arrangement of objects, cards, cloths etc.. used in show me approaches to supervision.

Management Supervision. The supervision of work by a manager in an organization to ensure quality of product or service. Although some managers may operate in a more person-centred way than this (particularly in service industries), the main task of the supervision is to ensure that the work is done well.

Modalities. Ways of exploring supervisory issues.

Monitoring. Ways of tracking time, energy, interest, investment within the supervisory session.

Mourning. The final stage in the life cycle of a group according to Tuckman and Jensen.

Narrative supervision. An approach to supervision which focuses on the storied nature of human experience, seeing human beings primarily as interpreters of those stories.

Normative. A term which derives from Inskipp and Proctor's three legged stool in which the focus is on the managerial aspects of supervision and on the boundary-setting capacities of the practitioner in their work.

Norming. The second stage in Tuckman's life cycle of a group, it describes the time when groups set their rules or norms together.

Notice. (First level of seeing) Observation without interpretation.

Organizational supervision. The supervision of an organization, company, Board or system in which stakeholders participate.

Parallel process. A dimension of counter-transference in which aspects of the there and then relationship are replayed unconsciously in the here and now of the supervisory space. A form of ***communication by impact,*** it is sometimes referred to as mirroring.

Participative. A form of group supervision in which the supervisor draws supervisees in to supervising each other. Also known as supervision *with* a group.

Peer supervision. A form of group supervision in which participants collaborate in supervising each other.

Performative. The fourth of Paterson's five seats on the sofa whose focus is on getting the job done effectively.

Pre-transference is a way of speaking about thoughts, feelings and sensations which arise in supervisors before they actually meet supervisees. These could arise from initial contact by email or phone or in the time just before a supervision session begins. Pre-transference is an impactful experience which arises from the unconscious.

Process model of supervision. An approach to supervision which identifies the various factors operating within it, e.g. Hawkins and Shohet's seven eyes, Paterson's Sat Nav..

Projection. The unconscious process whereby painful or other difficult feelings such as rage or vulnerability are disowned by an individual and ascribed to another as a way of avoiding the pain entailed in feeling them or acknowledging them as one's own.

Projective Identification. The unconscious process through which someone on the receiving end of the projection of vulnerable, hostile or other difficult feelings can experience (as a result of the interaction) those feelings as if they were their own. It results in an unconscious communication by impact. The recipient (if aware enough of the dynamics) comes to understand what the person projecting cannot bear to feel and gently offers what has been disowned back to them.

Psychodrama. An action method predominantly used in group work in which group members become therapeutic agents for others in the group. Developed by Jacob Moreno, psychodrama has strong elements of theatre, often conducted on a stage where props can be used to explore whatever an individual brings to the group.

Realise. Third level of seeing. That moment when the penny drops and we join the dots and make a connection.

Reflection. The process of slowing down the pace to seek meaning in what has happened, is happening or could happen.

Reflective Practice. The term indicates the importance of reflection on what work throws up for practitioners. It involves developing reflexive and reflective capacities.

Reflective. (Of a tool) an exercise to facilitate deep thought about the situations in which one is engaged. (Of a person) the capacity to thinking deeply about the situations in which one is engaged, involving taking responsibility for one's own actions, motivations and influence, questioning norms and structures and a willingness to stay with uncertainty and provisionality. It involves a high degree of reflexivity.

Reflexivity. The capacity to reflect on one's own approaches, feelings, pre-judgements, responses and identity. It goes beyond problem solving and seeks to come as close as possible to understanding how others experience oneself. It requires a willingness to be open to feedback and new ways of thinking and doing things. It goes beyond protocols and procedures to develop wisdom in handling complexity and ambiguity.

Restorative. A term which derives from Inskipp and Proctor's 3 legged stool in which the focus is on helping the supervisee to discharge emotion and reconnect with aspects of themselves with which they have lost touch.

Reverse parallel process. If parallel process describes how aspects of the client - practitioner relationship gets replayed in the practitioner – supervisor/group relationship, reverse parallel process describes how the practitioner can unconsciously replay the supervisor/group dynamics when working with the client.

Reviewing the session. A moment towards the end of the session when learning is named and participants prepare to head back to work.

Reviewing the supervisory relationship. The regular practice of taking stock of a group's life and health. Initial review could be after 4-6 sessions then as required but at least annually.

Role. A way of being (or the functioning form) a person takes in any given moment.

Role repertoire. Jacob Moreno distinguishes overdeveloped, underdeveloped or adequate roles that people play. Someone might have an overdeveloped role of carer or underdeveloped role of responsible citizen stemming from their childhood.

Role reversal. A technique in which someone changes places (reverses roles) with others or with an image or object in order to gain insight into their perspectives.

Sat Nav. Paterson's six process structure governing the supervision session (hosting & containing; eliciting & focusing; exploring & imagining; tracking & monitoring; bridging & enacting; reviewing & closing.)

Sculpt. A tableau or static presentation of an incident or situation achieved by positioning group members bodies and props to represent characters, emotional states etc..

Seven eyed model. Hawkins and Shohet's process framework which looks at the there and then of the practice relationship and the here and now of the supervisory relationship.

Small world. Mooli Lahad's term for a collection of figurines and objects which may be used in creative supervision.

Somatization. Literally, 'becoming bodily or embodied', it denotes a process whereby a person's unconscious thoughts or feelings come to be expressed in that person's body. A form of communication by impact, the supervisor or group members may sense in their own bodies the stiffness, pain or exhaustion of the supervisee.

Stakeholders in supervision. Those who have an interest in what happens in the work being supervised i.e. employers, professional bodies, managers etc..

Storming. The third stage in Tuckman's Life Cycle of a group. It describes the stage in a group's life when it tests its own power, authority and influence.

Style. Of groups it usually refers to the degree to which participants participate. See Authoritative, Cooperative, Participative.

Supervisee(s). The name given to practitioners when they meet to reflect on their work.

Supervisor. The name given to the practitioner who facilitates reflection on practice.

Supervisory issue. The material that supervisees explore in supervision.

Supervisory process. The overall name for the accompaniment offered to supervisees as they reflect on their work from arrival to departure.

Supervisory question. The focused form of the issue that supervisees want to explore in supervision.

Supervisory space. The physical environment in which supervision takes place whether in person or online; also refers to the time set aside for the session itself.

Team supervision. Group supervision in which all members of the group routinely work together and in which the objectives and dynamics of the team are explored as well as or instead of focusing on the work of individuals.Usually facilitated by a supervisor who may or may not be part of the team.

Three legged stool. A colloquial term used of Inskipp and Proctors 3 tasks of supervision: Normative, Formative, Restorative.

Three levels of seeing. I notice, I wonder, I realise as found in the Greek of John 20 in the Christian Scriptures. Also known as Contemplative Inquiry.

Tools of distillation. Techniques used for getting the work of the supervisee into the room or for helping the supervisee narrow their focus or get to the heart of the matter.

Tracking. The process of ensuring that the supervisory question and its focus is being pursued throughout the supervisory session.

Transference. A form of projection in which feelings and interactions originating in one relationship or setting are transferred onto another relationship or setting, such as the projection of feelings about authority figures onto care givers or supervisors.

Transformative. An extension of Inskipp and Proctor's Normative, Formative, Restorative tasks in which the focus is on what the supervisee is learning from practice.

Uni-professional supervision. The form of supervision in which both supervisor and supervisee inhabit the same discipline i.e. a teacher supervising a teacher, a youth worker a youth worker.

Verbatim. A way of bringing live work into supervision. It involves the practitioner writing as accurate a word for word account as they can remember of a live encounter from which they want to learn, and which they then explore with a supervisor or with others in a supervised group.

Wonder. Second level of seeing. Whatever arouses curiosity or to turn things over in our minds.

About the Authors

Michael Paterson is the Founding Director of the Institute of Pastoral Supervision and Reflective Practice. He first trained as a counselling supervisor and then, ten years later, as a Cross-Professional creative supervisor at the London Centre for Psychodrama. He is the co-architect (with Ewan Kelly) of *Values Based Reflective Practice* (VBRP) which supports frontline health and social care workers internationally.

Michael's publications include: *Enriching Ministry: Pastoral Supervision in Context* (2014) with Jessica Rose; *Pastoral Supervision: A Handbook* (2nd edition, 2015) with Jane Leach, *Between a Rock and a Hard Place: Pastoral Supervision Revisited and Revisioned* (2020) and *Pastoral Supervision: Creativity in Action* (2021) with Liz Crumlish.

Michael is the programme lead for the IPSRP Diploma in Cross-Professional Supervision, co-lead with Liz Crumlish on the IPSRP Diploma in Group Supervision and with Rebecca Loundar on the Graduate Diploma in Professional Supervision at Alphacrucis University College, Australia. Michael regularly leads supervision workshops in Australia, Europe and the UK.

Liz Crumlish has served in Health Care Chaplaincy and in Parish Ministry. For the last few years she has worked in renewal and pioneering, mentoring leaders and congregations through cultural change. Liz is a regular blogger offering biblical and theological reflections in poetic form www.liz-vicarofdibley.blogspot.com

She has contributed to various publications, including *There's a Woman in the Pulpit* Ed Martha Spong (2015) *Seeing Afresh: Learning from Fresh Expressions of Church* Ed David McCarthy (2019) and *Pastoral Supervision: Creativity in Action* with Michael Paterson. In 2022 she published *Stories of the*

Well: Recovering Her Story and *Birthing God – A Resource for Advent: Exploring the Women Named in Jesus' Genealogy.*

An associate of IPSRP, Liz teaches the Diploma in Cross-Professional Supervision and is co-lead with Michael Paterson on the Diploma in Group Supervision.

The Institute of Pastoral Supervision & Reflective Practice

Founded in 2008 by Michael Paterson and with Associates across the world,
The Institute of Pastoral Supervision & Reflective Practice
is an international community of practice
committed to training, writing and research in the field of supervision.

The Institute offers accredited training,
professional development,
consultancy and
individual and group supervision
online and in-person.

A full list of Associates and publications can be found at www.ipsrp.org.uk

Training in Group Supervision

The best preparation for becoming a Group Supervisor is to have been a supervisee in a well-facilitated supervision group.
The Institute of Pastoral Supervision & Reflective Practice (IPSRP) offers in person and online group supervision.
Further details from enquiries@ipsrp.org.uk

The Institute also runs a professionally accredited
Diploma in Group Supervision
which comprises of a residential intensive
plus a series of online practitioner workshops.
The course is currently on offer in the UK and in Australia.

The Institute also runs professional development and upskilling workshops in group supervision in-person and online.
See www.ipsrp.org.uk for latest information

Printed in Great Britain
by Amazon

21104076R00142